RAGE BAKING

RAGE BAKING

THE TRANSFORMATIVE POWER OF FLOUR, FURY, AND WOMEN'S VOICES

KATHY GUNST *and* **KATHERINE ALFORD**

PHOTOGRAPHY BY JERRELLE GUY

TILLER PRESS

NEW YORK   LONDON   TORONTO   SYDNEY   NEW DELHI

TILLER PRESS

An Imprint of Simon & Schuster, Inc.
1230 Avenue of the Americas
New York, NY 10020

First Tiller Press hardcover edition February 2020

TILLER PRESS and colophon are trademarks of Simon & Schuster, Inc.

For information about special discounts for bulk purchases, please contact
Simon & Schuster Special Sales at 1-866-506-1949 or business@simonandschuster.com.

The Simon & Schuster Speakers Bureau can bring authors to your live event. For more
information or to book an event, contact the Simon & Schuster Speakers Bureau
at 1-866-248-3049 or visit our website at www.simonspeakers.com.

Interior design by Patrick Sullivan and Jennifer Chung
Photography by Jerrelle Guy
Endpapers by Jim West / Alamy Stock Photo

Manufactured in the United States of America

3   5   7   9   10   8   6   4   2

Library of Congress Cataloging-in-Publication Data

Names: Gunst, Kathy, author. | Alford, Katherine, author.
Title: Rage baking : the transformative power of flour, fury, and women's voices
(a cookbook with more than 50 recipes) / Kathy Gunst and Katherine Alford ;
photography by Jerrelle Guy.
Description: First Tiller Press hardcover edition. | New York : Tiller Press, 2020. | Includes index.
Identifiers: LCCN 2019046205 (print) | LCCN 2019046206 (ebook) | ISBN 9781982132675 (hardcover)
| ISBN 9781982132682 (ebook)
Subjects: LCSH: Cookies. | Women political activists. | LCGFT: Cookbooks.
Classification: LCC TX772 .G87 2020 (print) | LCC TX772 (ebook) | DDC 641.86/54--dc23
LC record available at https://lccn.loc.gov/2019046205
LC ebook record available at https://lccn.loc.gov/2019046206

ISBN 978-1-9821-3267-5
ISBN 978-1-9821-3268-2 (ebook)

To Maya and Emma, my smart, beautiful daughters.
You give me hope. Let's keep working on making this world
a better place for women.

—KATHY GUNST

To Asher, who has taught me what real love and a
compassionate world should be.

—KATHERINE ALFORD

You should be angry. You must not be bitter. Bitterness is like cancer.
It eats upon the host. It doesn't do anything to the object of its displeasure.
So use that anger. You write it. You paint it. You dance it. You march it.
You vote it. You do everything about it. You talk it. Never stop talking it.

—MAYA ANGELOU

The truth will set you free, but first it will piss you off.

—GLORIA STEINEM

CONTENTS

*1961, "Ban the Bomb" March in front of the White House,
organized by Women's Strike for Peace*

FOREWORD

Stephanie Schriock
President of EMILY's List

I believe in the power of women in all of their roles.

After all, I'm the president of EMILY's List, an organization that has existed since 1985 to elect pro-choice Democratic women. Many people don't know that our name is based on a baking pun—EMILY isn't a person, it's an acronym. Early Money Is Like Yeast . . . it makes the dough rise. Created at a time when no Democratic woman had been elected to the Senate in her own right and there were fewer than twenty-five women in Congress, EMILY's List has since grown from a fund-raising organization into a powerhouse that has helped more than 1,200 women get elected to offices up and down the ballot. We train candidates, raise and donate money to support them, run independent expenditures, and work with women candidates through their wins and losses.

We've been around a long time and are proud of our success, but even we saw something different after Donald Trump got elected. Suddenly the number of women who reached out, looking for help running for office, skyrocketed. Women were marching, they were donating, they were knocking on doors and voting, and they were RUNNING FOR OFFICE. In 2018, we had our biggest election cycle, supporting more women than ever, including the twenty-four women who flipped Republican House seats (and, in turn, flipped the House and made a woman Speaker), the two new Democratic women senators, four new women governors, and literally hundreds of women in state and local offices around the country.

Despite that growth, women are still represented in less than 25 percent of Congress and hold less than a third of state legislative offices. And we still haven't cracked that hardest and highest glass ceiling of all—the White House. Which means here at EMILY's List, we can't let up, even a little.

So it was a natural fit when Kathy and Katherine got in touch about donating some of the proceeds of this amazing book to EMILY's List. We love the fact that some of your Rage Baking can help out women across the country, those running for the first time and those running for reelection, in their efforts to make their communities better.

Thank you for your support of EMILY's List and the amazing women we support. Let's all put our rage into both our baking and our activism, in whatever form that takes. As a veteran of many campaigns around the country, I can tell you that campaigns can always use both volunteers and baked goods. I hope you'll consider both.

INTRODUCTION

Kathy Gunst

I t was late September 2018. I was glued to the television. I listened all day as the Senate grilled Dr. Christine Blasey Ford about the "incident," as they called it, with Supreme Court nominee Brett Kavanaugh. I watched as Rachel Mitchell, a female prosecutor from Arizona, the woman puppet for the men in gray suits, asked the same questions over and over again.

I remember thinking: *Why is this called a "hearing?" No one is really listening to Dr. Ford.*

I kept asking myself: *Why would this woman risk her career, family, safety, and reputation to challenge a Supreme Court nominee if it never really happened?*

A line from a song in the musical *Hamilton* kept running through my head: "No one else was in the room where it happened."

And I remember thinking, toward the end of the "hearing," when it became clear that despite all the testimony, they would push Kavanaugh through: *Women don't get heard.* Women are considered hysterical if they sound the alarm over a man's bad behavior instead of accepting the old logic that "boys will be boys."

In a press conference after the hearing, Senator Lindsey Graham from South Carolina, told reporters, "I don't doubt something happened to her, but she is saying it's Brett Kavanaugh but she can't tell me the house, the city, the month, or the year . . . Ms. Ford is a very accomplished lady, something happened. I thought it was a good suggestion for her to go talk to someone and work through this."

I had a wonderful father. He was funny and smart, told wicked jokes (often at the expense of others), and was beloved by many. But that week, listening to the Kavanaugh hearings, I inadvertently hit the rewind button in my memory and heard my father reacting to me as a young girl, a teenager, and a young woman.

My father called me "Sarah Bernhardt" when he thought I was being overly dramatic. Sarah Bernhardt, a French actress in the late 1800s, gained fame for her emotional acting style. When I was in crisis (something as mundane as sparring junior high girlfriends or as complicated as having trouble with the Vietnam War), he always had the same line: "Okay, Sarah Bernhardt!" It was his code for telling me to take a breath, quiet down. But it almost never worked. His insistence that I be more ladylike, less full of opinion, was like lighter fluid on the fire. It made me want to roar.

Every woman I know has some version of this story.

That week, and the one after, when we watched Brett Kavanaugh sputter with anger, tongue jutting into the side of his mouth as he spilled and spun one story and sad excuse after another, I felt a level of rage that I rarely experience explode within me.

We were at a dinner party with close friends. And of course we were discussing the hearing. One of the men made a flip comment about the way women were reacting to what was happening in that Senate committee room, and, well, I lost it. I stormed away from the dinner table, locked myself in the bathroom like a teenager, and wept with fury. I stayed there longer than was socially acceptable. When I came back to the table, tear-soaked, I did what well-behaved women the world over do: *I* apologized for getting upset, for pulling a *Sarah Bernhardt*.

I read the editorials. I listened to NPR. And then "my" senator, Susan Collins of Maine, a supposed "moderate Republican," claimed she was holding off on her decision until she heard all of Dr. Blasey Ford's testimony. During that week, I will admit to calling Senator Collins's office more than once a day. I will come clean and say that the messages I left in the senator's voice mail were often quite heated; some might even call them "dramatic." I lost all hope in the senator who, it turned out, was secretly making deals off camera. (Months later, she received millions of out-of-state dollars for her upcoming 2020 campaign after she voted to confirm Kavanaugh. Senate Majority Leader Mitch McConnell, Republican from Kentucky, told Fox News, "Senator Collins will be well funded, I can assure you.")

When I watched Collins stand on the Senate floor telling us why she would vote yes for Kavanaugh's approval, I felt defeat for all women. What charged through my mind was the rant by the lead character in Paddy Chayefsky's seminal 1976 film *Network*: *I'm mad as hell and I'm not gonna take this anymore.*

My rage bubbled and seethed. This time, rather than tamping it down, politely changing the subject, or apologizing for being emotional, I listened to my rage. If I expected others to take me seriously, I needed to honor it, to hear this part of myself. But this anger at a system that pretends to listen to women threatened to take me over in a way that felt destructive.

I took long walks, but came back just as angry. I talked to like-minded friends but came away thinking: *We need to be talking to the other side*. Nothing worked to dispel my rage.

And then, late one night, I found myself in my kitchen, pulling flour, sugar, butter, and baking powder out of the pantry. I decided to bake a simple almond cake topped with late-summer fruit. I scooped out the flour and made sure it was perfectly level in my measuring cup. I softened the butter. I listened to the whole almonds growl as I chopped them in the blender. I peeled ripe peaches and caught every last drop of their sweet juice in my batter. I scattered the last of the tart, wild Maine blueberries on top. And a few hours later, I had a gorgeous cake and a calmer heart.

The next day, I returned to the kitchen and focused on creating tahini chocolate chip cookies and a mixed berry galette. The day after that, I melted chocolate and baked a flourless cake that offered the satisfaction of a brownie with the sophistication of a French tart. Strangely, I wasn't particularly interested in eating any of these creations. But I suddenly, *desperately*, wanted to spend long hours in the kitchen, baking and then baking some more.

The UPS man rang my doorbell with a delivery, and I handed him the cake and a batch of cookies. He looked at me with an expression that was both grateful and perplexed. I didn't even try to explain.

I took pictures of my baking and posted them on Instagram with the hashtag #ragebakers. Did I make the connection between my rage and this newfound interest in/obsession with baking? I'm honestly not sure, but it felt like something I *had* to do. Friends and strangers on social media reacted positively. "I feel the same way," many women wrote. "Baking sounds a lot better than lying on the couch weeping."

Did the baking stop the rage? Hell no. Did the baking make all the lies and deceit and behind-the-scenes dealings feel less menacing? Not one bit. Did the baking make me feel less afraid of the erosion of democracy I was witnessing as I listened to the evening news? No, it didn't really do any of those things.

What the baking did was reset my focus for a few short hours. It became a balm, a meditation of sorts. Baking was a way of temporarily restoring my belief in *the positive transformation of things*—in this case, butter, flour, sugar, and fruit. Each day, as the political outrages piled up, my mind was absorbed in the precision and focus and discipline that baking requires. A simple cake took me away from the news cycle. It was the calmest I'd felt since the Kavanaugh hearings were announced.

I suppose the other benefit of all this baking (besides the adoration of the UPS guy and several friends and neighbors who were thrilled at the sugary goods a worn-out, flour-splattered me delivered to their kitchens) was the way I felt strong enough to go back out into the world, refocused, regenerated, and ready to fight for the things I believe in.

I began to see parallels between baking and the state of the world. If I focused and stayed on task, my yeasty bread dough bubbled and rose in a productive way. My buttery pastry, after it chilled for the requisite time, didn't crack or fall apart. Baking helped me reset and figure out what my contribution to community, to activism, to political discourse might look like.

I marched. I wrote letters to my senators and congressmen and -women. I tried to soothe my adult daughters, who both called devastated at what they were witnessing. I gave donations to Planned Parenthood and organizations that fight for women's reproductive rights. I connected with women in Maine who were considering running against Susan Collins in the next election. Mostly, I tried to believe that what was happening in our country could still be fixed. I needed to convince myself and my daughters that the approval of Brett Kavanaugh's nomination to the Supreme Court did not mean that women would lose their rights.

But just a few months later, in May 2019, twenty-five white men in the Alabama State Senate voted to make abortion illegal even in cases of rape and incest. (The state's female Republican governor, Kay Ivey, signed it into law.) Other states followed suit. By the time you read this, I don't know what will have happened, what kind of rage you might be feeling.

The news keeps coming at us, like an unrelenting tornado. There is no time to truly absorb these stories, these outrages. We are like sponges that are already fully soaked. How are we to process the way these men are trying to turn back the clock, take away women's right to choose, tell us what we can and can't do with our own bodies?

Let me be clear: this is *not* a book telling women that if they get back into the kitchen and start baking, their rage will be sedated and all will be well. *Far from it.*

This is a book about women's voices, women's recipes, women in community with one another.

Don't let anyone tell you you're being too dramatic, too loud, too outspoken. Too *Sarah Bernhardt*. Speak out. Speak up.

Whether you march, make a donation large or small, work for a candidate you believe in, or join a local organization fighting for something that speaks to you, stay informed and involved. Now more than ever, our voices matter.

This is how we fight together. Protest together. Vote together. Make change together.

Let's make our voices heard, together.

When Katherine and I set out to write *Rage Baking*, we knew it had to be much more than a "regular" cookbook. As two women who have been in the food journalism/media world for many decades, we weren't quite sure what that might look like. So we did what felt natural and took it one step at a time. Our first step was to reach out to a community of women we respect and admire. Bakers, chefs, food writers, fiction and nonfiction and television writers, poets, artists, illustrators, musicians. And in no time at all, we had a wildly diverse group of women (over forty women from more than twenty states) responding with a resounding "Hell, yes!" It seems the connection between rage and baking, and the passion for cooking and activism casts a wide net.

This is the Rage Baking collection. You'll find over fifty recipes for cakes, pies, cookies, sweet and savory breads, candy, and granola, each with a story to tell. You'll also find essays and interviews, poems and illustrations. But what we hope you'll find, more than anything else, is inspiration. Inspiration to regain your equilibrium while you bake, inspiration from the powerful words the women in this collection share, and inspiration to get out there and fight for what you believe in.

The black-and-white photographs that open each of these chapters were taken by Nancy K. Rudolph (1923–2017). Nancy photographed all over the world, and these shots are part of a collection of a Women's Peace Demonstration in November 1980 at the Pentagon, organized by Women's Pentagon Action. Nancy was Kathy's mother-in-law. "I like to think that if Nancy were still here she would be thrilled to be part of this book and in the company of this incredible group of women," says Kathy.

RAGING INGREDIENTS

Baking powder and **baking soda** are chemical leaveners and essential for quick breads, cookies, and various cakes. They add lift and air (in the form of carbon dioxide) when they react with heat or moisture. Baking soda (sodium bicarbonate) is used in conjunction with something acidic, such as buttermilk, sour cream, vinegar, or natural (not Dutch-process) cocoa powder, and liquid in a recipe to stimulate the chemical reaction. Baking soda reacts when moistened and helps with texture, spread, and browning in cookies. Baking powder contains baking soda already mixed with an acid, such as cream of tartar, and cornstarch, to prevent clumping. Most baking powder sold today is double-acting, meaning it reacts both at room temperature when moistened and with heat. If you have ever made a batch of pancakes with baking powder, you may have noticed both the bubbles in the bowl and the lift the pancakes get when they hit the skillet. That is the double reaction in action. We prefer aluminum-free baking powder for its cleaner flavor. If you add too much chemical leavener in a recipe, it will have a tinny chemical aftertaste. (It probably goes without saying, but don't use baking soda that is being used to control odors in the fridge.) Both baking soda and baking powder lose potency over time, so it's important to make sure the leavener you're using is fresh. Check the "use by" date printed on the package. If you want to check the potency of your baking soda, put 1 tablespoon vinegar in a bowl and add ½ teaspoon baking soda; it should bubble up vigorously. If there's no reaction, it's time to replace it.

Butter is an essential ingredient in great baked goods. When beaten with sugar (known as creaming), it suspends air in the batter, resulting in light cakes; when chilled and lightly worked into flour for pie dough, it melts during baking to make flaky piecrusts. It enhances and delivers flavor in cookies and with chocolate, and a tablespoon or two softens the tartness in a lemon curd. We use unsalted butter unless otherwise specified. Buy a good-quality butter, such as those graded AA. Some bakers prefer to use high-fat European-style butters, which are cultured like yogurt and have a tart flavor. Oil, margarine, whipped butter, and butter–olive oil blends *should not be substituted* for standard butter in these recipes.

The temperature of butter is important to how it performs in a recipe. If chilled butter is called for, use it straight from the refrigerator. If a recipe calls for butter at room temperature, the butter should be soft to the touch—literally. If you press your finger into the butter, it should leave an imprint with just some resistance, like pressing into clay. If the butter looks greasy, it's too soft. There is no set amount of time to pull butter from the fridge—in winter you can remove butter from the refrigerator overnight, but on a hot summer day, it only takes a short time to soften, often just as long as it takes to pull the rest of the ingredients together. If you forget to remove butter from the fridge, it's tempting to microwave it for a bit to soften it, but this can result in melted butter in the center of a firm stick. If you must microwave, do it at 50 percent power and keep an eye on it. A better solution is to dice the butter and spread it out on a plate; the smaller pieces will come to room temperature relatively quickly.

We give measurements for butter in sticks: 1 stick = 8 tablespoons = ½ cup = 4 ounces.

Store butter well wrapped, away from other foods, especially cheese, onions, and fish, as it picks up odors easily. If not using within a couple of weeks, it's best to store butter in the freezer in an airtight container. Long-stored butter can develop a "fridge or freezer" taste that is off-putting.

Great **chocolate** is both a treat and a revelation. There are various types of chocolate that should be part of a baker's pantry. Unsweetened chocolate, often bought in 1-ounce squares, is 99% chocolate liquor (also called cacao), the essence of chocolate with *no added sugar*. It's intense and very bitter and is generally mixed with sugar in a recipe. It can be labeled as "bitter chocolate" or "baking chocolate." Semisweet and bittersweet chocolates vary in taste and sweetness and can range from 35 to 85% cacao; both are mixed with sugar, emulsifiers, and vanilla. Semisweet is generally sweeter, but there is no standard in the United States as to what is labeled "semisweet" or "bittersweet." One company's bittersweet may be comparable to another's semisweet. Generally we prefer chocolates with 50 to 65% cacao for baking. Almost all companies now list the cacao content on the packaging.

Chocolate chips vary from brand to brand, and are available in milk, dark, and white. There is also a difference between imitation and real chocolate chips, so be sure to check the label. Imitation chocolate chips don't contain cocoa butter, are blended with hydrogenated oils, and do not perform the same as real semi- or bittersweet chocolate in baked goods; do not substitute. If you want to make your own chips, coarsely chop a good-quality chocolate bar or block of chocolate. Quality chocolate bars suitable for baking can often be found in the candy section; look for a dark or semisweet bar chocolate with no added ingredients.

There has been a boom in artisanal chocolates in the United States, and the nuance of flavor found in fine chocolate is comparable to the qualities found in fine wines. We are fans of using artisanal chocolate baking chunks and disks for creamier texture and depth of flavor in cookies and cakes.

Chocolate should be stored, well wrapped, in a cool, dry spot, but not refrigerated. Use chocolate within six months of purchase.

Chocolate production has a dark history of both human and environmental exploitation. We advocate for reforms and support third-party certification for fair trade and sustainability. Labels on chocolate bars often list environmental and sustainability information.

Unsweetened cocoa powder is best for baking. There are two types of cocoa powder: natural and Dutch-process. Natural cocoa, also known as *nonalkalized*, is what most Americans grew up with. It is full-flavored, medium brown, and slightly bitter, and can be used in old-fashioned cakes, brownies, puddings, and shortbread. Natural cocoa is usually paired with baking soda as a leavener. Dutch-process cocoa has been treated by a process that neutralizes its acidity, and offers a mellower flavor. If a recipe specifies Dutch-process cocoa powder, it's part of the recipe's success, so don't substitute natural cocoa.

Citrus zest is the skin of a citrus fruit. Always wash and thoroughly dry your citrus before zesting. We prefer a Microplane for finely grating the zest of oranges, lemons, and limes. Be conscious of only zesting the colorful outer portion of the fruit's peel—don't get carried away and grate the bitter white pith below the zest. If the zest will be used to perfume simple syrup or the milk for a custard, use a vegetable peeler to remove the zest from the fruit in wide strips. When adding grated citrus zest to a cookie dough, cake batter, or pastry dough, first mix the zest in a small bowl with sugar. The sugar will absorb the oils from the citrus zest and make it easier to add the zest into your batters.

Cream cheese, **ricotta**, **yogurt**, and **crème fraîche** are cultured dairy products with a slight tang. We used standard supermarket brands when testing these recipes, but if you have a local brand that you love, go for it.

We use large **eggs** in all the recipes in this book. If you use extra-large eggs or smaller eggs, it will alter the results. Our preference is for organic cage-free eggs, and lately we are also making an effort not to buy eggs in plastic containers due to how landfills and oceans don't need any more plastic. (Once you start thinking about the impacts of sourcing, it's easy to feel like a character from *Portlandia*.) Eggs are often called for "at room temperature." If using eggs straight from the fridge, set the eggs in a bowl of warm tap water for about five minutes to bring them to room temperature before using.

We like to crack eggs into a separate bowl before adding them to batters or doughs. Why? Because if a bit of eggshell accidentally falls into a bowl of batter, it's a whole lot harder to retrieve than if it falls into a bowl of eggs. A quick tip: Use half an eggshell to scoop up any little pieces of shell that get away from you. It works every time.

We use unbleached all-purpose **flour** for most of the recipes in this book. When we call for "1 cup all-purpose flour," we are talking about *120 grams of flour* (see "Get Out That Scale"). Some recipes may call for cake, bread, pastry, whole wheat, or rye flour, or cornmeal—use the flour specified for the most successful results. This may seem fussy, but this is where the science of baking comes into play. One of the key differences between these flours is the amount of protein they contain. Protein, when moistened and then mixed or kneaded, turns to gluten, which is exactly what you want to give breads great structure, and exactly what you *don't* want for delicate cakes and pastries. Simply put, bread flour has the highest protein content and is well suited for chewy and crispy crusts; all-

Get Out That Scale

You may wonder why we give measurements for flour in both cups and grams. When we were testing the recipes for this book, we would test the same recipe but end up with different results. One day, after this had happened a few times, Katherine asked Kathy, "How are you measuring your flour?" Felt like kind of a personal question, but Kathy answered honestly: "Fill the measuring cup, tap it on the counter, and then use a kitchen knife to level it out." "Aha!" Katherine responded. Turns out, there are many ways to measure flour, and everyone is quite convinced theirs is the best.

*What to do? Get out the scale. We hate telling cooks to buy new equipment, but a modest kitchen scale can be indispensable and highly affordable. When a recipe calls for **1 cup flour**, we no longer guess if we hit it right—we simply place a bowl on top of our kitchen scale, calibrate the scale to zero, and fill the bowl until the scale tells us we're at **120 grams**. Bingo! Suddenly, we're all testing the same recipe and getting the same fabulous results.*

While we avoid the use of bathroom scales like the plague, this little baking/kitchen scale turns out to be quite handy, inexpensive, and unintimidating. So go on, get out your scale. It's going to be okay.

purpose flour is in the mid-range and tends to be our go-to flour; and cake flour has the least amount of protein, making it ideal for cakes and cupcakes. Having a range of flours in your pantry will definitely up your Rage Baking game. Very finely ground nuts, such as almonds or walnuts, are also referred to as flours, although they do not contain any wheat. Flour should be stored in a cool, dry, dark spot; if you only use it occasionally, it's best to store flour in the freezer.

There has been a recent explosion in regional, artisanal grains and organic flours. We support this movement for both its benefits to local economies and the improved flavor and freshness of these products. Many of these specialty flours can be found at farmers' markets or online (see Mail-Order Rage on page 163).

We use whole or 2% **milk**. We are major fans of **buttermilk** with its tart flavor and low 1 to 2% fat content. We count on it as a fridge staple, as it lasts for several weeks. It gives biscuits the fluffiest texture and helps add flavor and depth to cakes, pies, and quick breads. Whipping and heavy **cream** are interchangable. We prefer the flavor of just pasteurized versus ultra-pasteurized, but it's getting harder to find in the supermarket, and using ultra-pasteurized is not a deal-breaker. We don't like light cream for whipping. **Half-and-half** should be the real deal; nonfat half-and-half has no place here (or anywhere else, really).

Vegetable **oil** refers to a neutral-flavored oil, such as safflower or corn. Feel free to use what you have on hand, as long as it doesn't have a strong flavor. We are specific about extra-virgin olive oil. It doesn't have to be (nor should it be) the most expensive variety, but it should have a pronounced olive fruitiness. We use coconut oil. We prefer virgin coconut oil over the refined sort with its more pronounced coconut flavor.

Salt is essential to bringing out the flavor in baked goods. Even though a quarter teaspoon or a pinch may seem inconsequential, it's amazing how bland and flat a cookie or bread can taste if you leave it out. When in doubt, fine salt is best in baking, as it distributes evenly. We specify when a recipe needs kosher salt or another coarse salt. Flaky sea salt, like Maldon, is a wonderful finishing salt for cookies and bars.

We use granulated **sugar** unless otherwise specified. Brown sugars (we are specific about light or dark) bring both moisture and a molasses flavor to many recipes. Store brown sugar very tightly sealed at room temperature or in the freezer to avoid it becoming rock-hard after opening. If your brown sugar has hardened, simply transfer it to a bowl, drizzle with a teaspoon or two of water, cover with a paper towel, and microwave in twenty-second bursts, stirring after each, until soft. Some recipes call for other types of sugar, such as Demerara or turbinado. We make suggestions for substitutions when applicable. Confectioners' sugar is great for giving a sweet, snowy finish to cakes, cookies, and pies and is best sifted with a fine-mesh strainer before use. Confectioners' sugar is also a baker's friend when it comes to covering up any less than perfect results (wink wink). We also call for sanding and colored sugars, which are more widely available these days (thank you, Instagram). They are an easy way to add color and shine to cookies and cakes.

We prefer the full-bodied taste of pure **vanilla extract** versus imitation vanilla flavoring. We acknowledge that pure vanilla can be pricey, but we find it's totally worth it since a little bit goes such a long way. We love the perfume of vanilla paste and vanilla beans, but these are also pricey. If you have these in your pantry, feel free to substitute them for the vanilla extract called for in a recipe.

Yeast is essential in breads. Yeast is a single-cell living organism that feeds off the sugars in dough and releases CO_2 as a by-product, which causes the dough to rise and increase in size. We use two types of yeast: active dry and rapid-rise/instant. Both come in granulated form and are sold in jars and premeasured ¼-ounce packets. Active dry yeast needs to be hydrated or "proofed" in warm water (110°F) before it is mixed into a dough. Rapid-rise-instant yeast can be added directly to recipes without proofing. We prefer active dry yeast for doughs with longer rising like focaccia (page 70) and rapid-rise/instant yeast for sweet doughs like pull-apart bread (page 67). Yeast has a limited shelf life; always check the use-by date listed on the package.

RAGING EQUIPMENT

We recommend having a couple of sizes of rimmed aluminum **baking sheets** on hand: a half sheet pan is 18 x 13 inches (46 x 33 cm); a quarter sheet pan is 13 x 9 inches (33 x 23 cm). Rimless cookie sheets are nice to have, but if a recipe calls for a cookie sheet and you don't have one, simply turn a baking sheet over.

A **bench scraper**, also called a pastry scraper or bench knife, is a flat rectangular piece of metal or stiff plastic, often with a handle on top. We use this handy (inexpensive) little tool all the time when baking: to scrape up dough (particularly sticky, wet dough) that's stuck to a bowl or work surface, to push or scoop up dough or baking ingredients off a work surface, and to cut large pieces of dough into smaller portions. It can also be used much like a knife to cut up butter. It's a great tool for cleaning off a floured counter, as well. A curved plastic bowl scraper is also helpful when working with dough. We love these for cleaning out yeast dough stuck to the bottom of a bowl.

Having a selection of small, medium, and large stainless-steel **bowls** and glass bowls is super helpful. Small bowls come in handy for holding that teaspoon of baking soda, cinnamon, or salt. We don't love mixing in plastic bowls since they can pick up odors. We use soft rubber **spatulas** for mixing, offset ones for frosting and spreading, and have a good **knife** for chopping. A **rasp grater**, often referred to by the brand name Microplane, is great for zesting citrus or grating chocolate. A **pizza wheel** is useful for cutting dough.

We use a **Bundt pan** for many cakes. The ridged edges create a beautiful design. We call for a standard 9-inch round **cake pan** in

Read the Recipe First

It sounds like such basic advice, but you'd be amazed how many cooks ignore the crucial step of reading a recipe through before starting to bake. There's nothing worse than being halfway through a cake recipe only to learn that you need a pint of blueberries for the filling or that a cookie batter needs to rest overnight.

After more than twenty years running the Food Network Test Kitchen, Katherine is a huge advocate of what the pros call **mise en place** (French for "put in place"). This is simply a matter of pulling out all your ingredients and measuring them **before you start to bake**. Setting out all your ingredients on a pan or tray also makes cleanup easier. In many baking recipes, the combining of ingredients takes just minutes, and having everything ready makes your baking go much more smoothly. Added bonus: You will never again wonder if you actually added the salt or the baking soda. Simply look at your **mise en place** and see if it's still there.

many recipes; nonstick is great, but we still suggest lining the pan with parchment paper. For breads and loaf cakes, we use a 9 x 5-inch **loaf pan**. For all these pans, the heavier the metal gauge, the better. Darker pans will absorb more heat than lighter pans, making the bottoms of baked goods brown faster.

When cooling your baked goods, using a **wire rack** can make a big difference in the final product. Baked goods cooled directly on the counter can get soggy or continue to cook unevenly; a rack allows even airflow around the pan or baked good.

Stand mixers make easy work of creaming, beating, and mixing. We appreciate that a stand mixer is an expensive tool. However, Katherine's mixer is over thirty years old and Kathy's is over a decade, and both are going strong. (We only wish cars lasted that long.) A hand mixer can be used instead in many cases, but the mixing time may be longer, so use the visual cue in the recipe instead of the instructed mixing time. If you don't have a mixer when making bread, use a wooden spoon to mix, and enjoy kneading by hand.

It is important to have both dry and liquid **measuring cups** for accurate baking. Although a cup has the same volume in both dry and liquid measures, the risk of inaccuracies increases if you measure dry ingredients in a liquid measuring cup, it's easy to over fill.

When measuring liquids, place the measuring cup on the counter, lean down so the markings are at eye level, and watch for the ingredient to come to the desired line as you pour it in. We love liquid measuring cups, either glass or plastic, that can be read from above as well.

Dry measuring cups are calibrated to hold the exact amount: ¼ cup, ⅓ cup, ½ cup, ¾ cup, 1 cup, etc. Spoon the ingredient into the cup and drag a straight edge, such as a knife, an offset spatula, or a bench scraper, across the top to level off the ingredient. In most cases, it's best to avoid tapping the filled cup on the counter, which can cause the ingredient to settle and throw off the measurement. The exception is with brown sugars, which are usually tightly or loosely packed into the cup.

Measuring spoons work under the same principle as dry measuring cups: ingredients are added and leveled off for accuracy. It's important to buy measuring cups and spoons from reputable companies because it's not uncommon for cheaper products to be inaccurate.

Know your **oven** and **oven thermometers**. Over the years we've found that our ovens seemed off, sometimes by as much as 25° to 50°F. An oven's internal thermometer is only accurate in the location where it was installed, usually in the back or side of the oven. An oven thermometer is your best bet to get an accurate reading of your oven's true temperature. For best results place a thermometer on the center rack. When checking for doneness, always look for color or textural cues in a recipe and don't be a slave to the timing, as ovens do vary. Also, when checking for doneness, it's important to get in and out of the oven efficiently. Leaving the oven door open for even a short time can cool off the oven as much as 50°F and can alter accurate baking times. It's better to remove the item from the oven, close the door, check for doneness, and then return the item to the oven if longer baking is needed.

Position the oven racks for optimum baking: Cakes prefer the center of the oven. Piecrusts and pies should be baked in the lower third. For more than one sheet of cookies, adjust the racks so they're evenly spaced, and switch the baking sheets from top to bottom and vice versa about halfway through the baking time.

We like a **pastry brush** for brushing melted butter over a pan, spreading beaten egg or jam on a piecrust, or dusting off excess flour. Use only food-safe brushes, not those designed for paint.

Nine-inch metal or glass **pie plates** are both fine. Glass has the advantage of allowing you to see how a crust is baking on both top and bottom, while metal transmits heat faster.

We prefer the lightness of a French-style **rolling pin**, the tapered kind with no handles, but any type will do.

We are fans of cookie **scoops** and small ice cream scoops, which make easy work of forming cookies and icing cupcakes (see page 10).

Reusable and reliable **silicone baking mats** are great tools for lining baking pans. Cookies won't stick and they make cleanup easy. **Parchment paper** also works well and is essential for lining cake pans. Parchment comes in rolls or precut sheets. (See Mail-Order Rage on page 163.)

A GREENER KITCHEN

We are conscious of the amount of garbage we generate in the kitchen. Plastics—and single-use plastics, particularly—are a big problem. You will notice that we call for plastic wrap in some recipes, but you can always subsitute parchment or waxed paper, or look for reusable alternatives to plastic wrap, like Bee's Wrap (www.beeswrap.com) or reusable stretchy plastic lids. Clean out plastic bags and reuse them (nothing wrong here). There are also little things you can do when baking: When you unwrap a stick of butter, use the wrapper to butter pans and baking sheets as needed, then recycle the wrapper. Cover bowls with lids or plates versus single-use plastic wrap. Wash and reuse foil. Reuse takeout containers. A great way to transport cupcakes and cookies is in upside-down pint or quart containers: Put the cupcake on the inverted lid, cover with the container, and press down to seal. Stuff multiple reusable bags into your purse, backpack, or car to avoid having to use plastic grocery bags.

> *Use reusable alternatives to plastic wrap.*

It goes without saying to try and recycle glass, metal, and plastic (check with your local recycler for specifics). We try to compost all our organic and plant matter as well. If you have a backyard or live in the country (like Kathy), you can start a pile of compost near the garden or far from the house to avoid odors drifting into your kitchen. But if you don't garden, don't have the space to create a compost pile, or live in a city (like Katherine), you still have several options. Look for a local company that collects compost and turns it into organic soil; many companies that collect food waste from restaurants and private homes are popping up all over the country. Farmers' markets often collect scraps. Katherine has been known to take bags of compost on the subway to bring to a composting center.

> *Connect with a local company that collects compost and turns it into organic soil.*

Collect compost in an odor-proof lidded bucket or start a compost bag and keep it in your freezer (to avoid smells). When it's full, bring it to a composting center. Advocate with your local government to initiate composting for residential garbage collection.

1

SUGAR AND SPICE
and DONE BEING NICE:

COOKIES, BARS, AND BITES

RECIPE LIST

OATMEAL COOKIES

From Ruth Reichl

2½ cups instant oats

1 cup packed dark brown sugar

1 teaspoon baking powder

Pinch of fine salt

1 stick unsalted butter, melted, plus more for buttering

1 large egg, beaten

1 teaspoon pure vanilla extract

When food writer, memoirist, and editor Ruth Reichl sent us the recipe for these cookies, we worried we had a problem. They call for so few ingredients, and the recipe appeared so simple, that we figured they just couldn't be that special. But were we ever wrong.

"My mother's friend Hermine was the first feminist I ever knew," writes Ruth. "Unmarried—and happy about it—she was a career woman who did exactly what she liked in life. One of those things was cooking. She never arrived at our house without a carefully wrapped box of her homemade cookies. It was years before I realized that they were not something she had invented herself, but a great American classic."

These cookies are chewy and extremely delicate. And although they contain no nuts, the combination of butter, oats, and brown sugar gives them a distinctly nutty flavor. An added bonus: They are gluten-free.

Position racks in the upper and lower thirds of the oven and preheat the oven to 350°F. Brush two cookie sheets with butter.

Mix the oats, brown sugar, baking powder, and salt together in a medium bowl. Add the melted butter and stir together with a wooden spoon. Add the egg and vanilla and mix until evenly moistened.

Drop slightly heaping tablespoons of the batter onto the prepared pans and flatten them with the back of the spoon. Bake until the edges of the cookies begin to brown, about 8 minutes. Let the cookies sit on the cookie sheets for a minute or two, then use a metal spatula to transfer them to a wire rack and let cool completely. If they stick to the cookie sheets, put them back in the oven for a minute, then try again. These cookies will keep in a tightly sealed container for up to 5 days.

THE REVOLUTION
By TESS RAFFERTY
WILL BE CATERED

Here's the bad news, America: you've woken a white-hot atomic geyser of rage in women. Here's the good news: we've brought cookies.

By the time we got to June 2016, I was already fed up with the blatant and vicious sexism we were experiencing during the primaries, and that was just from within my own allegedly woke party. Somehow white men had reclaimed the word "progressive," redefining it to no longer include the goals of women. The misogyny was coming from inside the House. Of course, that was just an "amuse-douche" to what we would experience in the general election as chants of "Lock her up!" morphed into "Grab 'em by the pussy." In case the message that America doesn't really care about women was getting lost, having people decide it's okay for a man to talk to you that way as long as they get a tax cut really sells it.

And as bad as November 8, 2016, was, we knew it was only the beginning.

Gorsuch. Kavanaugh. Roy Moore. The Muslim travel ban. The transgender military ban. The abortion ban. A Möbius strip of attacks on the Affordable Care Act. Voter suppression in North Dakota. Voter suppression in Texas. Stacey Abrams having the election stolen from her like a mugging in broad daylight that bystanders don't want to get involved in. The outrages pile up like the layers of a chocolate trifle. We can't even fully experience the despair and anger of one event before the next one is already happening.

I have become a turducken of rage. I am "rage at the men in my life who need to do better" stuffed in the "rage at the men in my party who claim to be an ally but still judge us on a curve" stuffed in the "rage at the Republicans who want to legislate us into *The Handmaid's Tale* while they let Putin be their campaign manager." I am anger wrapped in hopelessness wrapped in despair wrapped in more anger. A lot more anger.

And when I can't stand it anymore, I cook.

Baking is a good distraction: it prevents you from hitting refresh on both your browser and your outrage. It gives your mind a focus besides constantly wondering if you'll ever sleep through the night again. You can't afford to not be present while you're measuring out 2¾ teaspoons of salt or wielding a knife: that will make for some awful-tasting cookies and at least one trip to urgent care. By being present while the oven heats up, we avoid getting heated up by our being present.

Women have never been more energized to fight back: We make calls, we protest, we run for office. We volunteer and fund-raise and register voters. We are doing everything we can today to create a different tomorrow. But a "different tomorrow" can be hard to quantify and so much of what we do is send our energy out into the ether, never really knowing what its effect is, or if it even had one. The nice thing about baking is that you can actually see the results. You have a tangible product for your efforts, one that tastes delicious and fulfills our most basic needs: *sustenance*. And we all need something to sustain us right now.

But it's not just our bodies or our mental health that we are sustaining when we hit the snooze button on the news cycle and hit a ball of bread dough instead. We are also sustaining this movement. Taking the time we need to refuel allows us to wake up and fight another day with renewed energy and spirit. And so our rage fuels our cooking and our cooking fuels our rage.

DROP DEAD!
PECAN SPICE COOKIES

From Betty Fussell

2 cups (240 grams) all-purpose flour

1½ teaspoons baking soda

1½ teaspoons ground cinnamon

1 teaspoon ground ginger

¾ teaspoon freshly grated nutmeg

½ teaspoon ground cloves

½ teaspoon fine salt

Freshly ground black pepper (optional)

1⅓ cups pecans, finely chopped

1 stick unsalted butter, at room temperature

½ cup packed light brown sugar

½ cup molasses

1 teaspoon pure vanilla extract

1 large egg, beaten

¼ to ⅓ cup granulated sugar or sanding sugar

"Because I like to improvise and play with whatever I'm cooking, I'm not a good baker," admits ninety-two-year-old cookbook author and memoirist Betty Fussell. "Especially if I'm in a rage and seek the kitchen for outlet. Impatient with precise measurement at the best of times, rage requires a foolproof classic that I can't ruin. I resort to a traditional drop cookie of sugar-butter-flour-nuts-spice that I can push onto the baking pan from the tip of a spoon. Got no patience for rolling out dough and fiddling with a cookie cutter in this kind of mood. Obviously I will (just as you will) ad-just spices in quantity and kind. If I'm really mad, a dash of black pepper in the dough does me no end of good."

Whisk together the flour, baking soda, cinnamon, ginger, nutmeg, cloves, salt, and some pepper, if you like, in large bowl. Stir in the pecans.

In a stand mixer fitted with the paddle attachment, beat the butter and brown sugar on medium speed until light and fluffy, about 1 minute. Add the molasses and vanilla and beat until fully incorporated. Add the egg and beat until evenly combined. With the mixer on low speed, add the flour mixture and beat until just incorporated. Cover and refrigerate until the dough is firm enough to scoop, about 30 minutes.

Position two racks evenly in the oven and preheat the oven to 375°F. Line two baking sheets with parchment paper or silicone baking mats.

Put the granulated sugar on a plate. Scoop up about 2 tablespoons of the dough and roll it into a ball, then roll the ball in the sugar to coat. Place it on the prepared bak-ing sheet and repeat with the remaining dough, spacing the cookies about 2 inches apart. Using your hand, press down on the cookies to flatten them.

Bake the cookies until slightly puffed up and just crisp along the edges, 12 to 14 minutes, switching the pans from top to bottom and bottom to top about halfway through the baking time. Transfer the baking sheet to a wire rack and let cool. These cookies will keep in a tightly sealed container for up to 5 days.

TAHINI CHOCOLATE CHIP COOKIES

From Kathy Gunst

1 cup plus 2 tablespoons (130 grams) all-purpose flour

¾ teaspoon baking soda

A generous pinch of Maldon or other sea salt, plus more for sprinkling

1 stick unsalted butter, at room temperature

½ cup tahini, well stirred

⅓ cup granulated sugar

⅓ cup packed light brown sugar

1 large egg, at room temperature

1 large egg yolk

1 teaspoon pure vanilla extract

1 (10- to 12-ounce) bag bittersweet or semisweet chocolate chunks, chopped, or chocolate chips (about 1¾ cups)

About ¼ cup white sesame seeds

Chocolate chip cookies are everywhere. And while I never tire of a good chocolate chip cookie, I wanted to take this classic to the next level. So I added tahini (roasted ground hulled sesame paste) and it hit the perfect note. The cookies are not overly sweet, and the tahini gives them a rich, nutty flavor, much like peanut butter but far more interesting. A sprinkling of crunchy toasted white sesame seeds and coarse sea salt is the perfect finishing touch. The dough can be refrigerated for at least four days or frozen for up to two months.

Mix the flour, baking soda, and salt together in a small bowl.

Beat the butter, tahini, granulated sugar, and brown sugar on medium speed in an electric mixer or in a stand mixer fitted with the paddle attachment for about 3 minutes, until fluffy and fully incorporated, stopping and scraping down the sides of the bowl a few times as needed. Add the egg, egg yolk, and vanilla and mix for 1 minute more.

With the mixer on low speed, gradually add the flour mixture and mix until just combined. Remove the bowl from the mixer and, using a rubber spatula, fold in the chocolate, being careful not to overmix. Cover the dough and refrigerate for at least 1 hour or up to overnight. (This might sound fussy, but the cookies are honestly better after the dough has had a chance to rest.)

Position two racks evenly in the oven and preheat the oven to 325°F. Line two baking sheets with parchment paper or silicone baking mats.

Scoop out a generous tablespoon of the dough, roll it into a ball, and place it on the prepared pan, making sure not to place the cookies too close together. Repeat with the remaining dough, dividing the cookies between the prepared pans. Lightly moisten your palm and gently push the cookies down to flatten them. Sprinkle with the sesame seeds and press them lightly to make sure they adhere to the dough.

continued

Bake for 6 minutes, then rotate the pans 180 degrees and switch their positions from top to bottom and bottom to top. Bake for 6 to 8 minutes more, until the cookies are almost deep golden brown around the edges, but still somewhat pale in the center. Remove from the oven and sprinkle the cookies with the sea salt, gently pressing it into the cookies to adhere.

Let the cookies cool for at least 5 minutes on a wire rack then serve slightly warm or at room temperature. Store in a tightly sealed container at room temperature for up to 2 days.

COOKIE TIPS

*E*ver wonder why the simplest of all baked goods—cookies—can sometimes be amazing and other times not so impressive? We've learned a few things about how to make your cookies come out perfect every time.

WHEN A COOKIE RECIPE CALLS FOR BUTTER "at room temperature," it should be somewhat soft to the touch but still firm. You don't want butter that is a puddle of almost-melted mess.

WHEN COOKIE RECIPES CALL FOR MIXING BUTTER AND SUGAR until tender and light, here's what we're looking for: In a stand mixer (usually fitted with the paddle attachment) or in a large bowl using a handheld mixer, beat the butter and sugar until the sugar is no longer grainy, 3 to 5 minutes. This is known as creaming, and it creates air bubbles that help give the dough structure. This will help you bake cookies that are tender and light.

THE REASON SO MANY COOKIE RECIPES CALL FOR ADDING THE EGGS ONE AT A TIME is that eggs will not emulsify properly with the fat in the butter if they're added all at once. And if the first egg isn't emulsified with the butter and sugar before the next one is added, it could break down the batter.

COOKIE DOUGH IS ALWAYS BETTER AFTER IT CHILLS—anywhere from an hour to overnight. Store it in an airtight container in the refrigerator. If you think this is just a fussy step, try baking one batch immediately and then bake a batch after the dough has had a chance to chill and rest. The cookies that were refrigerated will be noticeably better.

WHEN ADDING CHOCOLATE CHIPS, NUTS, OR OTHER CHUNKY INGREDIENTS TO COOKIE DOUGH, fold them in by hand with a rubber spatula so you don't overwork the dough.

USE A COOKIE OR ICE CREAM SCOOP, ¼-cup or ⅓-cup dry measuring cup, or large kitchen spoon for uniformly sized cookies.

LINE YOUR COOKIE SHEETS with a sheet of parchment paper or a silicone baking mat to make cleanup easier and also to provide a layer of insulation between the pan and the cookies, which tends to give you more uniformly baked cookies.

IF YOUR COOKIES ARE BROWNING TOO QUICKLY on the bottom, slip another pan underneath to insulate.

NEVER CROWD THE COOKIE SHEET. Cookies—particularly ones made with lots of butter—spread out as they bake. Space them about 2 inches apart on the pan before baking.

WHEN BAKING MORE THAN ONE SHEET OF COOKIES AT A TIME, always rotate the sheets halfway through baking. All ovens have hot spots, and rotating the pans ensures more even baking. Rotate the baking sheets 180 degrees, and if you have multiple sheets in the oven at the same time, switch their positions, moving the one on the top or center rack to the bottom and vice versa.

WHEN BAKING A BIG BATCH OF COOKIES, always let the pans cool before preparing the next batch. Baking cookies on a hot cookie sheet will melt your dough and throw off the baking time.

WHEN YOUR COOKIES ARE DONE BAKING, let them sit on the cookie sheet for a few minutes before transferring them to a wire rack. As they sit, they firm up, making it easier to remove them from the pan.

STORAGE TIPS: Store cookies in an airtight container—a cookie tin or a resealable container or bag—at room temperature for up to 3 days. Unbaked cookie dough can be stored in an airtight container for up to 1 week or frozen for several months.

MARBLED CHOCOLATE-AND-VANILLA COOKIES

From Katherine Alford

2½ cups (300 grams) all-purpose flour

½ teaspoon baking powder

½ teaspoon fine salt

¼ teaspoon baking soda

2 ounces bittersweet chocolate, chopped, or about ⅓ cup bittersweet chocolate chips

2 sticks unsalted butter, at room temperature

2 tablespoons unsweetened Dutch-process cocoa powder, sifted if clumpy

½ teaspoon ground cinnamon

1½ cups sugar

1 large egg

2 teaspoons pure vanilla extract, or ½ teaspoon pure almond extract

Why choose between vanilla and chocolate? These playful cookies combine a vanilla dough and a chocolate dough in a patchwork quilt pattern. It's way simpler than it sounds. Drop spoonfuls of the dough onto a piece of plastic or reusable wrap, roll it up like a party favor, chill, then slice. The result? A delish, impressive-looking, swirly black-and-white cookie without a lot of fuss.

Whisk the flour, baking powder, salt, and baking soda in a medium bowl.

Put the chocolate and 3 tablespoons of the butter in a heatproof medium bowl and set it over a small saucepan of barely simmering water (make sure the bottom of the bowl doesn't touch the water). Stir until melted and combined, about 2 minutes. (Alternatively, put the chocolate and butter in a microwave-safe bowl and microwave in 20-second bursts, stirring after each, until melted and combined.) Whisk the cocoa powder and cinnamon into the melted chocolate until smooth. Set aside to cool slightly.

In a stand mixer fitted with the paddle attachment, beat the remaining butter and the sugar on medium-high speed until light and fluffy, about 3 minutes. Add the egg and vanilla and beat until combined, stopping to scrape down the sides of the bowl as needed. With the mixer on low speed, add the flour mixture and beat until combined.

Divide the dough evenly in half (about 380 grams per piece). Return half the dough to the mixer bowl and transfer the other half to a separate bowl. Add the melted chocolate mixture to the dough in the mixer bowl and beat until smooth.

Lay out a large piece of plastic or reusable wrap or parchment paper on your work surface. Drop alternating heaping tablespoons of the dough—one chocolate and one vanilla—onto the plastic to make a rough patchwork quilt, about 11 × 3 inches long. Use the plastic to roll the dough into a tight log, then twist the ends tightly like a party favor to compact the dough. (For larger cookies, don't roll the dough quite so tight so you have a fatter log.) Refrigerate until firm, about 2 hours or up to overnight.

continued

Position racks in the upper and lower thirds of the oven and preheat the oven to 350°F. Line two baking sheets with parchment paper or silicone mats.

Slice the dough into ½-inch-thick rounds and place them about 2 inches apart on the prepared pans.

Bake the cookies until the edges are golden, 15 to 20 minutes, switching the pans halfway through. Let cool on the pans for about 5 minutes, then transfer to wire racks to cool. These cookies will keep for 3 days in a sealed container.

PEANUT BUTTER STICKY FINGERPRINT COOKIES

From Karen Duffy

1 cup smooth or chunky peanut butter

1 cup sugar

1 large egg

1 to 2 tablespoons raspberry preserves or your favorite fruit preserves.

"I love these peanut butter cookies, and have been making them ever since my sister Kate and I spent hours baking culinary miniature oddities beneath a 100-watt lightbulb. Our Easy-Bake Oven ignited my domestic curiosity," writes Duffy, a writer, model, and actress. *"This is the recipe I bake the most, share the most, enjoy the most. It is ridiculously easy—even easier than my Easy-Bake Oven treats."* If you spray the measuring cup with oil before measuring the peanut butter, it will slide right out.

Position a rack in the center of the oven and preheat the oven to 350°F. Line a baking sheet with a silicone baking mat or parchment paper.

Mix the peanut butter, sugar, and egg together in a medium bowl with a wooden spoon. It will be a sticky dough.

Roll the dough into 1-inch balls by hand and place them on the prepared pan, spacing them evenly. Press your thumb into each ball to make a shallow well. Fill each cookie with about ¼ teaspoon of the preserves.

Bake until the cookies are set and the edges are slightly brown, about 12 minutes. Let cool on the pan for 5 minutes, then transfer to a wire rack to cool. Store in an airtight container for up to 3 days.

BUFFY THE VAMPIRE SLAYER, MAD MEN,

AND A GRIST MILL

A CONVERSATION WITH MARTI NOXON

Martha (Marti) Mills Noxon is a partner and co-owner of Grist & Toll, a whole-grain flour mill in Pasadena, California. She is best known as the creative force behind several acclaimed TV series that feature strong female characters including Buffy the Vampire Slayer, *a series she wrote and for which she was executive producer. Other credits include* Mad Men, Glee, *and* Grey's Anatomy. *More recently, she created the critically acclaimed HBO limited series* Sharp Objects *and AMC's* Dietland. *She also created the hit shows* Girlfriends' Guide to Divorce *for Bravo and Lifetime's* UnREAL, *which earned her an Emmy nomination for Outstanding Writing for a Drama Series in 2016.*

KATHY GUNST: What does "Rage Baking" mean to you?

MARTI NOXON: I don't really associate baking with rage. I'm a textbook WASP. We don't rage. We do cocktails. (I don't drink anymore; I'm now a sober person.) A lot of women I know don't even know they're having rage. All of a sudden they'll be like, "Cakes! Anxiety! Fear!" Give me a self-soothing activity. And baking is such a self-soothing activity.

KATHY: Until it comes out wrong!

MARTI: I don't even mind when it comes out wrong. Full disclosure: Through a series of silly

> "I believe one of the reasons stories are tools for social change . . . is that stories can make people who are not necessarily empathetic put themselves in the shoes of the character and come back and say, 'Oh, I get it now.'"

events, I was up for casting for a television competition baking show. I got up to the round where they taste your stuff and I didn't have a lot of time to prepare. You know, I have a full-time job [as a writer]. So, I took a few days off and I baked so hard. But it didn't work out. I have baked on and off throughout my life. Baking is the perfect combination of self-soothing and perfectionism. Smells good, tastes good. For a perfectionist, the result can be pleasing.

KATHY: Do you still bake a lot?

MARTI: I baked a lot in my early life and then stopped for years because I didn't have the time. Once I had some disposable income and children, I started baking again. My daughter and I bake together a lot. I feel kind of passionate about it again. But man, it's expensive to bake.

KATHY: Yeah, tell me about it. You should see my bills for sugar and butter!

MARTI: Ha. I baked a carrot cake recently. I added up how much it cost, and that carrot cake cost me thirty-five dollars. Then you factor in the time it took away from me earning a living and that was like a fifty-dollar carrot cake!

KATHY: So how did you come to be an owner of Grist and Toll, greater Los Angeles's first grist mill in over one hundred years?

MARTI: I got kind of passionate about it again in my early forties. I was traveling for work and I was standing in line to get into some trendy restaurant and I started talking to this woman. She said she was a professional baker at a restaurant in the Valley. And I thought, *I've got to know you!* We became acquaintances, and soon after we met she ended up leaving her job. I told her I always wanted to invest in something bakery-related. But I didn't want to open another bakery. There are so many in L.A. And she said, "I've always wanted to open a flour mill." I didn't know what she was talking about. I thought flour came from the flour fairies. I started learning about whole grains, heritage grain, millers, and how overprocessed most American grain is. I became a grain nerd. I have deep and useless knowledge. [*laughs*] I told her, "Let's do it!" and that's how I became an owner of a flour mill. We imported an artisanal wooden mill from Germany. We source our grain meticulously.

KATHY: Does owning a flour mill ever inform the television and film writing you do?

MARTI: I think the most important thing I bring to my craft as a writer is specificity. What . . . people respond to is the deeply investigative, a sense that what they're watching feels real. It feels like I know what I'm talking about. When I write about divorce or anorexia, these are subjects very close to my own life, not research. Writing requires you to go deeper and be more specific than you can imagine. And with the mill I had to learn so much about grain. Why a mill must be properly ventilated, why whole grain is important . . . all that stuff shows up in my writing.

KATHY: Speaking of your writing, your female protagonists are fierce, and almost always angry. Can we talk about that? Let's start with Buffy the Vampire Slayer. She's a blond high school girl trying to save the world. A feminist hero.

MARTI: Buffy is the invention of a feminist man, Joss Whedon [a producer and the writer of Buffy]. I know him well, and Joss and I are not great at anger. One of the things it would be interesting to explore in the new Buffy is anger, how cathartic it is for a young woman to be able to release her anger, how satisfying.

KATHY: You once said, "I envy friends who grew up with a better handle of self-expression and anger." Was there no screaming in your childhood home?

MARTI: Zero. We are really good drinkers, Olympic-level drinkers.

KATHY: Now that you don't drink, how do you rage?

MARTI: Ha, can I get back to you on that? I'm still working on that. I think a lot of it comes down to my writing. *Dietland* [a darkly comedic series about women's body issues and misogyny] was a cosmic howl of rage. That was an angry show.

KATHY: You don't turn on the TV all that much and see a show about the deeply troubling world of anorexia and women's relationships to food and the way women's bodies are depicted in glossy magazines.

MARTI: Ha. It's such a niche show, made for feminist bakers in Maine.

KATHY: I mean, men are dropping dead and falling out of the sky on *Dietland*! You talked about "women changing the world one person at a time." Seems like such a reaction to the #MeToo movement?

MARTI: I was in a van scouting for *Dietland* when I got a call about the Harvey Weinstein story breaking. This was a show where almost everyone working on it were women—the director, crew, producers. The world was fucking going crazy. When I was pitching *Dietland* we thought Hillary Clinton was going to be our next president. This should be relevant. Such a funhouse mirror. In the end, the world was crazier than *Dietland*.

KATHY: When you're writing, do you know, or do you care, if your audience is politically in line with you? Does the audience's point of view matter?

MARTI: I believe one of the reasons stories are tools for social change, one of the reasons I endeavor so hard to make my work commercial, is that stories can make people who are not necessarily empathetic put themselves in the shoes of the character and come back and say, "Oh, I get it now." If I'm successful after you've watched *Girlfriends' Guide to Divorce* or *Dietland* or *Sharp Objects*, you think, *Wow, it must be so hard to be a woman with a family like that and not hurt yourself.* Or you think, *I always thought addicts are weak. But that woman is strong. Maybe I don't have it right.*

KATHY: Like Camille [the protagonist] in *Sharp Objects*? She is so deeply vulnerable and yet so determined.

MARTI: Right. The next time you encounter a woman and think, *I smell booze on her breath*, instead of thinking, *She's not reliable*, you might think, *Maybe I should ask her what's going on and see if she needs help?*

KATHY: In talking about *Mad Men*, which admittedly took place in a different era, you said, "Women are trying to find a place at the table with the big boys." You've been very successful in an industry that is *so* male dominated. What advice would you give young women?

MARTI: My hope for young women is that they don't have to do what I had to do. I never had to use sex for access, but I had to trade sexuality, trade being attractive and appealing and not being confrontational.

KATHY: I mean, Trump has been accused by dozens of women of sexual harassment and rape!

MARTI: We live in a culture where without proof, when it's his word against your word, women are always going to lose. It is heart-wrenching that we have to hear these stories and see these women discredited.

KATHY: Let's end on an up note. What fills you with hope these days?

MARTI: There's a lot of things that fill me with hope. Number one is young women. They are so fucking fierce. If anyone can fix this world, it's going to be them.

RAINBOW COOKIES

From Katherine Alford

1 large egg

½ teaspoon pure vanilla extract or almond extract

Pinch of salt

All-purpose flour, for dusting

1 (7-ounce) sheet frozen puff pastry, preferably all-butter, thawed*

1 to 2 tablespoons very finely chopped blanched almonds

About 1 teaspoon each purple, blue, green, yellow, orange, and red sanding or sparkling sugars

2 tablespoons granulated sugar (optional)

Thanks, Instagram, for making colorful pastries and sugars a thing! These cookies are quick to make and a great way to honor our LGBTQ+ sons, daughters, sisters, brothers, friends, parents, military, police, teachers, clergy, immigrants, elected officials, athletes, journalists, and so many more. As a trans parent, I appreciate the need for a Pride Day, or month, but honestly, I am proud every day. Don't limit these colorful, easy-to-bake cookies to just one day a year.

Beat the egg, vanilla, and salt together in a small bowl.

On a lightly floured surface, roll the puff pastry into a 12 x 7-inch rectangle. Arrange the pastry with one long edge facing you. Brush the surface of the pastry with some of the egg mixture. Scatter the almonds evenly over the surface of the pastry.

Starting about 1 inch from the far edge of the pastry, evenly sprinkle a ¾-inch-wide band of purple sugar horizontally across the pastry. Leave about a scant ¼-inch space uncovered, then sprinkle a band of blue sugar. Leave another small space, then repeat to make bands of green, yellow, orange, and red sugar. (You are creating a colored flag with a tiny bit of space between each stripe of color.) Starting with the red end, roll the pastry up into a tight log and pinch the seam to seal. Transfer the log to a pan or plate and put it in the freezer to firm up, about 10 minutes.

Lightly brush the outside of the log with the egg mixture and sprinkle with granulated sugar, if desired. Use a sharp knife to slice the log crosswise into ½-inch-wide cookies and lay them flat on the prepared baking sheet, spacing them evenly. Freeze until firm, at least 15 minutes.

Position a rack in the center of the oven and preheat the oven to 400°F. Line a baking sheet with parchment paper or a silicone baking mat.

Bake for 5 minutes, then remove the pan from the oven and reduce the oven temperature to 350°F. Using a metal spatula, flip each cookie, then return the pan to the oven and bake until puffed and golden brown, about 10 minutes more. Transfer to a wire rack to cool.

---

* Try to use an all-butter puff pastry. We love Dufour Classic Puff Pastry, which can be found in supermarkets and specialty markets in the frozen foods section.

CHOCOLATE RASPBERRY RUGELACH

From Kathy Gunst

2 cups (240 grams) all-purpose flour

Pinch of fine salt

8 ounces cream cheese, cut into cubes, at room temperature

2 sticks unsalted butter, cut into cubes, at room temperature

¼ cup sour cream

About 3 tablespoons cherry or raspberry jam

1 cup semisweet chocolate chips, or 6 ounces semisweet chocolate, coarsely chopped

1 cup raspberries, halved or quartered if large

3 tablespoons granulated sugar

Confectioners' sugar, for dusting

These chocolate-and-raspberry-filled crescents are extra moist thanks to cream cheese and sour cream in the dough. They are filled with chopped semisweet chocolate and fresh raspberries. Experiment with various fillings: try chopped toasted nuts with cinnamon-ginger sugar, or chopped fresh cherries and dark chocolate.

Put the flour and salt in a food processor and pulse to combine. Add the cream cheese and butter and pulse until the mixture is slightly creamy and thoroughly combined, about 15 pulses. Add the sour cream and pulse until well incorporated and the dough comes together. Turn the dough out of the food processor and divide it into 3 equal pieces (about 240 grams each). Shape each piece into a disk and wrap them individually in plastic or reusable wrap or waxed paper. Refrigerate until firm, at least 1 hour and up to 24 hours.

Line two baking sheets with silicone baking mats or parchment paper and set aside.

Working on a lightly floured surface, roll one disk of the dough into a 9- to 10-inch-wide circle (see page 145 for tips on rolling dough into a perfect circle). Using a pastry brush, brush off any excess flour. Brush the dough with 1 tablespoon of the jam and then scatter a third of the chocolate on top and press it lightly into the dough to adhere. Then add a third of the raspberries, gently pressing them into the dough, and sprinkle with 1 tablespoon of the granulated sugar.

Using a sharp knife or a pizza wheel, cut the circle into quarters. Cut each quarter into 3 equal triangles (like slices of pizza). Roll each slice from the wide end toward the narrow point. Place the rugelach on the prepared baking sheet, seam-side down. Repeat with the remaining dough, chocolate, and raspberries. Refrigerate for 20 to 30 minutes before baking.

Position racks in the upper and lower thirds of the oven and preheat the oven to 350°F.

continued

Bake the rugelach for 12 minutes, then switch the pans from top to bottom and bottom to top. Bake for 14 to 18 minutes more, until the rugelach are golden brown and the chocolate has melted. Let cool on the baking sheets thoroughly, then dust with confectioners' sugar and serve. Store in an airtight container for up to 5 days.

CHOCOLATE CHERRY BISCOTTI

From Grace Young

2 cups (240 grams) all-purpose flour

1 cup sugar

⅓ cup unsweetened Dutch-process cocoa powder

1½ teaspoons baking powder

¾ teaspoon fine salt

½ stick unsalted butter, cut into small pieces and chilled

2 large eggs

1 teaspoon pure vanilla extract

1¼ cups semisweet chocolate chips, preferably 60% cacao

½ cup dried cherries, coarsely chopped if large

Coarse sea salt (optional)

"I love these because they are rich and satisfying and made without a lot of fat," says wok guru Grace Young. *"And the dark chocolate and dried cherries are loaded with antioxidants and nutrients."*

Position a rack in the center of the oven and preheat the oven to 350°F. Line a baking sheet with parchment paper or a silicone baking mat.

Sift the flour, sugar, cocoa powder, baking powder, and salt into a large bowl. Add the butter and, using your hands or a pastry blender, blend in the butter until the mixture resembles coarse cornmeal.

In a small bowl, whisk the eggs with the vanilla; add the egg mixture to the dry ingredients and stir with a wooden spoon until just blended. Mix in ¾ cup of the chocolate chips and the dried cherries.

Generously flour a clean work surface. Using floured hands, divide the dough in half and shape each half into a 10 x 2-inch log. Transfer to the prepared baking sheet, placing them at least 2 inches apart and not too close to the sides of the pan (the dough spreads as it bakes). Bake for 30 minutes, or until the logs are firm when pressed with a fingertip. Let cool, about 45 minutes. Reduce the oven temperature to 300°F.

Transfer the cooled logs to a cutting board and use a serrated knife to slice them crosswise into ½-inch-thick biscotti. You should have around 22 biscotti. Arrange the slices on the same baking sheet, cut-side down, and bake for 15 minutes. Gently flip the biscotti. Bake for 15 minutes more, or until the biscotti are firm to the touch. Cool completely on a wire rack.

Meanwhile, melt the remaining ½ cup chocolate chips in a heatproof medium bowl set over a saucepan of barely simmering water. Stir until the chocolate is melted and smooth.

Set the rack over a piece of parchment or waxed paper. Using the tines of a fork, drizzle the melted chocolate over the cookies. Let the chocolate cool completely and set, about 1 hour. Store in an airtight container at room temperature for up to 1 week.

RUM RAISIN BROWNIES

From Julia Turshen

Cooking spray

¼ cup dark rum

½ cup raisins

3 ounces unsweetened chocolate, coarsely chopped

1 stick unsalted butter, cut into cubes

1 cup sugar

2 large eggs

½ teaspoon kosher salt

¾ cup (90 grams) all-purpose flour

According to cookbook author and activist Julia Turshen, "The best part about baking is sharing what you make and using it as a way to bring people together—whether you're headed to a rally, to celebrate a victory or a loss, to soothe an ache, to grieve a loss, or to simply just be together and remind one another that we care."

Soaking raisins in rum may seem like a simple step, but it adds a whole new dimension to chocolate brownies. Top with your favorite ice cream for a delicious brownie à la mode.

Position a rack in the center of the oven and preheat the oven to 350°F. Line an 8-inch square baking pan with parchment paper, leaving a couple of inches of parchment overhanging the sides. Mist the parchment with cooking spray.

Put the rum in a small saucepan and bring to just a boil over high heat (if the rum flames, don't worry, just wait a few seconds and then cover the pan with a lid). Remove from the heat, stir in the raisins, and let cool to room temperature.

Meanwhile, put the chocolate and butter in a heatproof medium bowl and set the bowl over a small saucepan of barely simmering water (make sure the bottom of the bowl doesn't touch the water). Stir the chocolate and butter until melted and combined, about 2 minutes. (Alternatively, put the chocolate and butter in a microwave-safe bowl and microwave in 20-second bursts, stirring after each, until melted and combined.)

Whisk the sugar, eggs, and salt into the chocolate mixture. Use a rubber spatula to stir the rum-raisin mixture into the batter, then add the flour and mix briefly to just combine. Scrape the batter into the prepared pan and smooth the top. Bake until a toothpick inserted into the center of the brownies doesn't have runny batter attached to it, 20 to 25 minutes. Let the brownies cool to room temperature, then use the overhanging parchment to lift them from the pan and set them on a cutting board. Cut into 16 squares. Store in an airtight container for up to 3 days.

CHOCOLATE CHOCOLATE CHIP COOKIES
with **HAZELNUTS**

From Katherine Alford

2 cups (240 grams) all-purpose flour

½ cup unsweetened Dutch-process cocoa powder

3 tablespoons malted milk powder, chocolate malt powder, or milk powder

1¼ teaspoons fine salt

1 teaspoon baking powder

½ teaspoon baking soda

2 sticks unsalted butter, at room temperature

1 cup granulated sugar

1 cup packed light brown sugar

3 large eggs, beaten

1 tablespoon pure vanilla extract

16 ounces mixed dark, milk, and white chocolate disks, chunks, or chips (about 2⅓ cups)

¾ cup hazelnuts, coarsely chopped

Milk powder is the secret ingredient of many experienced bakers, making cookies more tender and giving quick-rising breads more depth of flavor. Malted milk with its toasted flavor is a natural complement to the dark, milk, and white chocolates. Personal preference rules when it comes to chocolate chip cookies, whether you prefer them crisp, cakey, or chewy. These have crisp edges with a soft center when baked for the lower range of time and become crisp all through if you bake them longer. The batter benefits from resting for at least four hours and up to twenty-four hours before baking. This makes a big batch of cookies, and the good news is that the balls of dough freeze beautifully and can be baked straight from the freezer when you need a serious chocolate fix (these days, sadly, that's too often after the evening news). These cookies make awesome ice cream sandwiches—just sandwich slightly softened vanilla ice cream (or your favorite flavor) between two cookies. If you'd like to assemble ice cream sandwiches ahead, wrap them tightly in plastic or reusable wrap and freeze for up to four hours before serving.

Whisk together the flour, cocoa powder, milk powder, salt, baking powder and baking soda in a medium bowl.

Beat the butter and both sugars in a stand mixer fitted with the paddle attachment on medium-low speed until light and fluffy, about 2 minutes. Add the eggs one at a time, beating until each is incorporated before adding the next, then add the vanilla and beat until light, 3 minutes more.

Stop the mixer and add the flour mixture, then mix slowly until evenly incorporated. Add the chocolate and nuts and mix until just combined. Transfer the dough to a container, cover, and refrigerate for at least 4 hours and up to 24 hours.

Position two racks evenly in the oven and preheat the oven to 350°F. Line two baking sheets with silicone baking mats or parchment paper.

continued

Scoop 2 tablespoons of the dough (a slightly heaping 1½-tablespoon scoop is great for this), roll it into a ball, and place it on one of the prepared pans. Repeat until you have about 8 cookies on each pan, evenly spaced about 2 inches apart.

Bake until the cookies are set but still a little soft in the center, 12 to 15 minutes, rotating the pans halfway through the baking time. Let cool on the pans for a couple of minutes, then use a metal spatula to transfer the cookies to a wire rack to cool. Let the pans cool, then repeat with the remaining dough. Store in an airtight container for up to 5 days.

Will RAGE BAKING Help?

By CHARLOTTE DRUCKMAN

ONE WRITER ISN'T SO SURE

I'm not so sure about Rage Baking. I believe in rage. My faith in baking is unshakable—even if my technique is shaky. But Rage Baking?

I don't bake out of rage. When I'm angry, I tend to channel it into my work—to think about what I can write and then write it. When I've finished writing, or tired my constantly whirring brain looking for the right word or passable transition sentence, I bake to clear my head and get my sedentary self up from my laptop. I bake to feel like I'm physically engaging in a process that yields tangible results and has a clear start and end.

I love the act of smudging butter into flour, the cold fat spreading across my fingertips and falling back into the bowl. Sometimes I run my hands through the flour, just because. And have you ever watched butter melt? Or, if you take it further, sputter and foam, until it goes still, depositing brown bits of toasty sediment? What place is there for ire amid all this pleasure?

Baking gives me clarity. So does rage, but while the former serves as a kind of meditative practice, the latter gives me heightened, sharp focus. Anger motivates me, gets the brain back to churning, now on a fixed point. My rage is not blind. It strikes with measure and reason. And I would not want baking to get in its way—to temper or distract it, to empty my thoughts when they are at their most lucid, and powerful.

Like the feminist journalist Rebecca Traister, author of *Good and Mad* (see page 52), I believe in harnessing our rage and using it to change things—to empower ourselves and get things done outside the kitchen. I'm not sure how I feel about telling women to take their anger and get back in the kitchen and start making pies. If you can do that to create a world where we're not *expected* to bake pie, or where men would also take to their stand mixers when irate or to fight the good fight, that would make the whole thing worth it. But is that what Rage Baking is doing? I don't know.

I'm writing this—if not entirely on board with the whole baking-while-livid thing—under the assumption that if you've bought this book, you've done so not only because you want to bake (or are enraged), but also because you believe in the mission of EMILY's List: to put more female candidates in office. It's a wonderful synchronicity; the special interests line up, and that's great. But let's not kid ourselves. Buying the book is a show of support for baking and for women's advancement (bonus points if you bought it while angry—see, also, rage shopping), but now that it's in your hands, making one of the cakes, cookies, or pies found in these pages while experiencing any emotion isn't putting any more money into anyone's coffers except those of the grocer you procured your ingredients from or the coffers of the Domino sugar folks. (I am also under the assumption that everyone uses Domino sugar.)

Listen, if everyone was moved to bake for a cause whenever they got pissed off, post a photo of it on Instagram with all the requisite hashtags (#ragebakers), and send $100 to EMILY's List, I'd be telling us all to get really, really angry. But I don't see that happening anytime soon.

Just recently the state of Georgia passed what's known as a fetal heartbeat bill, which ostensibly bans abortion after only six weeks of pregnancy, dealing yet another blow to women's reproductive rights, and to women in general. Was I angry? You betcha. Did I bake? Nope. Did anyone? Who knows? If they did, it doesn't seem to have done a blessed thing, far as I can tell.

Maybe you remember how close the Georgia governor's election was—how Stacey Abrams was forced to concede to Brian Kemp in November 2018; how people still believe she was robbed. Guess who signed that bill into existence? Kemp. If Abrams had gotten just a few more votes, many of us would have one less thing to be angry about. Whoever baked a batch of shortbread to assuage their anger yesterday might not have eaten so many cookies. Maybe those cookies could have done more good sold at a huge bake sale to fund-raise or campaign for Abrams. Or not. Maybe it wasn't about cookies at all. Maybe if we spent less time coping with our rage by beating a ton of egg whites for a soufflé and more time speaking up and getting the vote out, we wouldn't have quite so much to be riled up about.

So, yeah, I guess what I'm saying is: Women (men too), take your rage to the streets, to the blogs, to social media, to your local and national representatives and politicians. Better still, consider running for office (hi, EMILY). Band together. And if you need to focus so you can channel that rage, well, yes, *maybe bake*. If you can take that rage and sell millions and millions of cookies and cakes to make enough money to really get things done (change policies, give agencies that stand up to the bad guys enough funding to do it successfully), bake. And if baking together might be a way we can pool our anger and figure out how to act collectively and inclusively, then, yes, bake.

LEMON BARS

From Vallery Lomas

For the Crust

Cooking spray

1¼ cups (150 grams) all-purpose flour

⅓ cup confectioners' sugar

¼ teaspoon fine salt

1¼ sticks unsalted butter, melted

1 teaspoon lemon extract (optional)

For the Filling

4 large eggs

1½ cups granulated sugar

Finely grated zest of 3 lemons
(about 1 heaping tablespoon)

½ cup fresh lemon juice
(from about 3 large lemons)

¼ cup (30 grams) all-purpose flour

½ teaspoon baking powder

½ teaspoon fine salt

Confectioners' sugar, for dusting

"I was born and raised in Baton Rouge—a food paradise where there was no shortage of fresh berries or cakes made by my grandmothers," Vallery Lomas tells us. "I was starting my final year of law school as the recession loomed, so I started a food blog, Foodie in New York, as a creative outlet.

"I worked as an attorney for eight years, and my passion for food and sharing recipes and stories persisted. A casting director for The Great American Baking Show discovered my Instagram account and urged me to audition for the 2017 season. I put my life on hold for several months as I prepared to compete and then went to England to film the show. And then I actually won! But my win never aired because the network canceled the show mid-season due to allegations of sexual harassment against one of the judges. I was most disappointed that my win would not have the effect of inspiring the next generation of curly haired, melanin-rich little girls as I hoped it would. However, I now realize that my presence in the often homogenous world of food media can still inspire people.

"Making lemon curd out of lemons has become my mantra. Lemon curd is a perfect metaphor for life: no matter how sour something is, add a little sugar and eggs, have patience, and work, and you will transform those lemons into something rich and delicious!"

These lemon bars are bursting with tangy, lemony flavor, but what's unique and brilliant about them is that Vallery figured out a way to make the curd without spending time cooking it on the stovetop.

Make the crust: Position a rack in the center of the oven and preheat the oven to 350°F. Line an 8-inch square baking pan with two rectangles of parchment paper, overlapping them so they are perpendicular to each other and leaving a couple of inches of parchment overhanging the sides. Give the parchment a quick mist of cooking spray.

Whisk together the flour, confectioners' sugar, and salt, in a large bowl. Stir in the melted butter and lemon extract (if using) until combined. Use your hands to press the mixture over the bottom of the prepared pan in an even layer. Bake for 15 minutes.

Meanwhile, make the filling: In a medium bowl using a handheld mixer, beat the eggs on medium speed until light and foamy. Sprinkle in the granulated sugar and beat until the mixture is pale yellow, light, and voluminous, 3 to 4 minutes. Reduce the speed to low and whisk in the lemon zest, lemon juice, flour, baking powder, and salt.

Pour the filling into the hot crust (no need to let it cool). Bake for 25 to 28 minutes, until the filling is lightly browned on top and doesn't appear wet or jiggle when you gently shake the pan. Set the pan on a wire rack and let cool to room temperature, then refrigerate for at least 1 hour or freeze for 30 minutes before serving.

Using the overhanging parchment, gently lift the lemon bars out of the pan and transfer to a cutting board. Cut into 12 squares (they are quite rich). Dust with confectioners' sugar just before serving. These are best devoured the day they're made.

CHOCOLATE PISTACHIO BUTTERCRUNCH

From Kathy Gunst

2 sticks unsalted butter

1 cup sugar

1 tablespoon light corn syrup

2 tablespoons water

8 ounces semisweet chocolate, 60% cacao preferred

About 1 cup *very finely* chopped pistachios or other nuts

This is the stuff of dreams, a crunchy, sweet, caramel candy coated in chocolate and nuts. I know what you're thinking: Isn't candy really hard to make? And the answer is no! My sister-in-law, Andrea Gunst, shared this buttercrunch recipe with me years ago, and it forever changed our holiday traditions.

You can double the recipe if you like, but if you want to make more than that you shouldn't try to multiply the recipe by three or four—simply keep doubling the recipe.

Line a baking sheet with a silicone baking mat or aluminum foil (if using foil, butter it well with butter or oil).

In a heavy-bottomed medium saucepan, combine the butter, sugar, corn syrup, and water and heat over medium-low heat, stirring frequently. Attach a candy thermometer to the side of the pan, raise the heat to medium-high, and cook, stirring frequently, until the mixture caramelizes and hits 290°F on the candy thermometer, at least 15 to 20 minutes. *Watch it carefully*, particularly toward the end of the cooking process. The mixture can burn easily; reduce the heat to very low and stir continuously if it seems to be cooking too quickly or turning darker than pale golden brown.

When the mixture hits 290°F, remove the saucepan from the heat and, working quickly, use a heatproof silicone spatula to carefully spread it in an even layer on the prepared pan. Let cool and harden.

While the buttercrunch is cooling, melt the chocolate in a small saucepan over *very low* heat, stirring until smooth.

When the buttercrunch is hard to the touch (you shouldn't feel any soft spots), use another spatula to spread a thin layer of the melted chocolate over the entire surface.

Sprinkle half the nuts onto the soft chocolate, pressing them down lightly so they adhere. Let the chocolate set until fully dry, with no wet spots. Carefully remove the candy from the mat or the foil and gently flip it. Spread the remaining chocolate over the surface of the buttercrunch

continued

and sprinkle with the remaining nuts, pressing them down lightly to adhere. Set the pan in a cool spot and let the chocolate harden.

When the chocolate is completely dry and hardened, use your hands to crack and break the buttercrunch into small pieces. Store in a cookie tin or tightly sealed container in a cool, dry spot for 2 weeks.

BAKLAWA

From Reem Assil

For the Syrup

1⅓ cups sugar

⅔ cup water

1 teaspoon fresh lemon juice
(from about ½ lemon)

2 teaspoons orange blossom water

2 teaspoons rose water

For the Nut Filling

3 cups walnuts (about 10 ounces)

¾ cup sugar

1 teaspoon ground cinnamon

1 tablespoon orange blossom water

1 tablespoon rose water

To Assemble

1 cup clarified butter or ghee, melted*

1 (16-ounce) package phyllo (or filo)
dough, thawed if frozen

*See recipe on page 34.

Reem's Bakery in Oakland brings together the flavors of an Arabic corner bakery with a commitment to community, social justice, and sustainability. Reem is a baker, chef, and activist. "Baklawa is a rite of passage for any Arab looking to impress a crowd," she tells us. "And everyone will swear that theirs is the original baklava, referring to the Greek version, which most Americans know. I love it as a topic of conversation and always joke that it embodies my spirit: delicately layered, nutty, and sweet! Making baklawa is simple and straightforward. But it does take precision and patience because it requires you to delicately handle each sheet of thin phyllo dough and brush it with butter. (It can be quite therapeutic!) This sweet delicacy can also be adapted to your taste and can include other fillings such as pistachios, almonds, even chocolate!"

Make the syrup: In a small saucepan, combine the sugar and water and bring to a boil over medium heat; reduce the heat to low and simmer until the syrup thickens enough to coat the back of a spoon, about 5 minutes. Remove from the heat and stir in the lemon juice, orange blossom water, and rose water. Let cool.

Position a rack in the center of the oven and preheat the oven to 350°F.

Make the nut filling: In a food processor, combine the walnuts, sugar, and cinnamon and pulse into fine crumbs. Drizzle in the orange blossom water and rose water and pulse until the mixture is evenly damp but not too pasty.

To assemble the baklawa: Put the clarified butter in a small bowl or measuring cup. Line a jelly-roll pan or 13 x 9-inch baking pan with parchment paper and, using a pastry brush, coat the parchment with butter.

On a clean work surface, unroll the phyllo and position it so one long edge is facing you. Cut the stack of phyllo sheets down the middle vertically, making sure the pieces fit into your prepared pan. Cover half the stack with a clean kitchen towel to prevent the phyllo from drying out. (Phyllo can dry out and tear, but because baklawa has so many layers, it is very forgiving and each layer does not have to be perfect.)

continued

Lay a sheet of phyllo in the pan and brush it generously with the butter, then repeat until you have used *half* the cut phyllo sheets. Scatter the filling over the phyllo and lightly pat it down into an even layer. Layer the remaining phyllo sheets over the filling, buttering each one before adding the next. Brush the top sheet of phyllo generously with butter.

With a sharp knife, cut the baklawa into approximately 2-inch squares, then cut each square in half diagonally to make triangles. (Make sure your knife cuts fully down to the bottom of the pan, gently placing your other hand on the top layer of phyllo to hold it in place as you cut.) Ladle any remaining butter over the phyllo, letting it fall into the cuts.

Bake until golden brown, 30 to 35 minutes. Let cool for 10 minutes, then pour 1 cup of the syrup evenly over the top. Let the baklawa cool to room temperature.

Clarifying Butter

Clarified butter is important for the success of a perfectly baked baklawa because it has a higher smoke point and allows the bakwala to turn a beautiful golden brown hue when baked. What's key about clarified butter is that the water has been removed, which helps keep the phyllo crispy and not soggy. It couldn't be simpler to make at home.

To make about 1 cup clarified butter, melt 2½ sticks butter in a medium saucepan over medium heat. Heat until the butter begins to bubble, a layer of white foam forms on top, and the milk solids sink to the bottom, then remove from the heat. Let cool to room temperature and settle, about 30 minutes. Once the butter has settled, carefully skim off the white foam on top and ladle the clear, golden butter into a storage container, leaving the milk solids at the bottom of the pot. Store clarified butter in an airtight container in the refrigerator for up to 3 weeks or freeze for 2 to 3 months. If you don't have time to clarify your butter, use store-bought clarified butter or ghee (which is clarified butter that has been cooked just a bit longer to brown the milk solids).

PIGS IN A BLANKET

From Kathy Gunst

8 ounces uncooked (Mexican) chorizo or hot Italian sausage links

1 teaspoon olive oil

All-purpose flour, for dusting

7 ounces frozen puff pastry, thawed (see page 19)

1 to 2 tablespoons Dijon mustard, plus more for serving

1 large egg or egg white

Sesame seeds

There are so many I could dedicate this recipe to, but especially "deserving" are the Republican men of the Alabama State Senate (and the state's Republican woman governor) who made it their mission to take away women's reproductive rights in 2019. Stuff some spicy chorizo sausage into premade puff pastry, roll tight, and bake in a hot oven until crisp, and golden brown. Bite hard.

Put the sausage in a small skillet and cover with 1 cup water. Bring to a boil over high heat, then cover and cook for 5 minutes. Drain the water. Return the pan to medium-high heat, add the oil, and cook the sausage, turning it to brown on all sides, about 1 minute on each side. Remove from the heat and let cool. Cut the sausage into 8 pieces.

Working on a lightly floured surface, cut the pastry into 2 equal pieces. Roll each piece into a rectangle about 9 x 5½ inches. Using a pizza wheel, cut each rectangle on the diagonal into 4 equal triangles.

Line a baking sheet with parchment paper or a silicone baking mat. Brush one pastry triangle with a touch of the mustard. Place a piece of the sausage at the base of the triangle and roll the pastry up toward the narrowest point. Place on the prepared baking sheet, seam-side down. Repeat with the remaining pastry, mustard, and sausage. (At this point, the pastry-wrapped sausages can be covered loosely and refrigerated for up to 2 hours before baking.)

Position a rack in the center of the oven and preheat the oven to 375°F.

Beat the egg in a small bowl. Brush the pastry with the egg and then sprinkle with the sesame seeds. Bake until the pastry is puffed and golden brown, 16 to 18 minutes. Serve hot or warm, with mustard for dipping.

2

Whisk, Fold, Knead,
RISE UP:

BREADS

RECIPE LIST

BUTTERMILK BISCUITS

From Maxine Siu

2½ cups (300 grams) all-purpose flour, plus more for dusting

3 tablespoons sugar

1½ teaspoons baking powder

1½ teaspoons kosher salt

¾ teaspoon baking soda

1½ sticks unsalted butter, cut into small cubes and chilled

1 cup cold buttermilk

About ¼ cup heavy cream, for brushing

Plow in Potrero Hill is one of San Francisco's most beloved breakfast spots. These biscuits are just one of the reasons customers are willing to wait in line for more than an hour to get a table. According to Maxine Siu, who owns Plow with her husband, "Growing up, one of my favorite breakfast dishes was biscuits and gravy. More often than not I would find the biscuits to be too dense and flavorless. So upon opening Plow, I set out to make a version I could be proud of. The biscuits started off as a weekend offering, but after some time we would get requests for them every day. This biscuit has become our most popular baked item."

Plow's biscuits are flaky and buttery. But what's even more extraordinary about them is their crisp texture on both the top and bottom. The secret? Lots of butter. A nice coating of cream on top. And baking them in a cast-iron or other heavy skillet. A 12-inch cast-iron skillet is ideal for holding all ten biscuits, but if you only have a 10-inch skillet, you can bake eight biscuits at a time and bake the extra two biscuits on a cookie sheet.

Serve them with eggs, omelets, bacon, sausage and gravy, or use them as the base for a breakfast egg sandwich, BLT, or any sandwich. Or serve them hot from the oven with honey butter (1 tablespoon room-temperature butter mixed with 1 tablespoon honey). They can also be served for dessert—split open and fill with vanilla-scented whipped cream and fresh berries. Or combine fresh fruit in a skillet, top with the raw biscuits, and bake until golden brown for a biscuit-topped fruit cobbler.

Position a rack in the center of the oven and preheat the oven to 425°F.

Whisk the flour, sugar, baking powder, salt, and baking soda in a large bowl. Using a pastry cutter or your fingers, work the butter into the flour mixture until the butter cubes are the size of lima beans or peas. Pour the buttermilk over the flour mixture and mix with a wooden spoon, to just combine, then knead until a shaggy dough begins to form.

Turn the dough out onto a lightly floured work surface and shape it into a rectangle. Fold it in half and then fold in half again. Repeat this two or three more times.

Using a well-floured rolling pin, gently roll the dough into a 10 x 8-inch rectangle between ½ and ¾ inch thick. Use a 2½-inch biscuit cutter, sharp knife, or pizza wheel to cut 8 biscuits from the dough. Gather the scraps and roll them into a rectangle between ½ and ¾ inch thick and cut out 2 more biscuits, for a total of 10. Tuck all 10 biscuits into a 12-inch cast-iron or other heavy oven-safe skillet, placing them right up next to each other with one or two in the center (see the headnote for tips on using a 10-inch skillet). Brush each biscuit with the cream.

Bake until golden brown, about 25 minutes. Let cool for a minute, then separate the biscuits and serve hot.

The biscuits can be made, cut, wrapped, and frozen for up to 1 month. Bake them straight from the freezer for about 28 minutes.

RYE GINGER SCONES

From Andrea Reusing

2 cups (240 grams) light rye flour

1 cup (120 grams) pastry flour

¾ cup turbinado or packed light brown sugar, plus about ¼ cup for topping

1½ teaspoons baking powder

¾ teaspoon fine salt

½ teaspoon baking soda

1½ sticks unsalted butter, cut into cubes and chilled

½ cup cold heavy cream

¼ cup cold crème fraîche

¼ cup candied stem ginger, drained (syrup reserved for brushing) and minced

Andrea is a James Beard Award–winning chef and food activist. For these delicious hybrid shortbread-scones she uses locally raised grains milled at Carolina Ground in Asheville, North Carolina (see Mail-Order Rage on page 163). Their light rye flour is both delicate and flavorful and pairs wonderfully with ginger. Searching out ginger root in syrup is worth the effort (see Mail-Order Rage on page 163); it adds both a potent ginger flavor and moisture to the mix, and the syrup is great for sweetening tea or drizzling over ice cream or berries. The scones are pressed, cut, and baked in a pan like a shortbread, resulting in a pleasing, crisp texture. Andrea serves these for breakfast, but they are just as good any time of day. She recommends keeping the cubed butter in the freezer until ready to use.

Whisk the rye flour, pastry flour, the ¾ cup sugar, the baking powder, salt, and baking soda in a large bowl to combine. Add the butter and, using your fingers, quickly work it into the flour mixture until the butter is in pea-size pieces.

Stir together the cream, crème fraîche, and ginger, in a medium bowl. Pour the cream mixture over the flour mixture and mix until the dough just comes together. The dough can be a bit powdery and is best worked by hand to make sure it is evenly mixed. Press the dough evenly into a 12 x 8 x ½-inch baking pan. Cover and freeze for at least 1 hour 30 minutes or up to overnight.

When ready to bake, preheat the oven to 350°F.

Leaving the dough in the pan, cut it into 8 squares and then cut each square diagonally into triangles. Sprinkle the top with the ¼ cup sugar. Bake on the center rack until puffed and golden brown, 25 to 35 minutes. (Gently push down on a scone; when they're ready, they shouldn't feel super soft or pillowy.) Let cool in the pan for 15 minutes, then re-cut the scones along your original cuts to separate them, if needed, and transfer to a wire rack to cool. Brush each scone with some of the reserved ginger syrup. Store in an airtight container for up to 2 days.

HURRICANE BEULAH

By HALI BEY RAMDENE

It was always summer in North Carolina. Houses only had screen doors, the magnolia trees—each and every one my mother would point out on the drive there—were always heavy with white and pink-tinged flowers, and in the small yellow house on Tyrell Street, Beulah Graham Teal was always cooking furiously upon news of our arrival. After sixteen hours of driving, we'd pour out of the van and into the heat of this always-summer. I'd turn and look at my mom to see her settle into this slower, girlish part of herself. I knew she was excited to be back home in Greensboro, excited for the cornbread she knew her mother had waiting for her, straight out of the oven. My father, the first to reach the door, knew there would be something for him, too. Beef stew. No matter what time of day, Beulah would have the stew ready for him. And for us, me and my brothers, my grandmother made the food "I know your mother doesn't feed you *up there*." This is what she'd say as she placed plates full of baked macaroni and cheese and collard greens before us.

This is the portrait of our first meal in North Carolina after the impossibly long drive from Albany, New York. My mother sitting with the warm cast-iron skillet of cornbread made especially for her, my father tucked into a bowl of beef stew ladled over grits, and my brothers and me squeezed between them at a small round table eating this creamy, cheesy macaroni that we absolutely *never* ate at home. After the meal, a glass bowl of banana pudding appeared—the recipe, followed word for word, from the back of a box of Nilla wafers. My mom always said she hated bananas, but she never seemed to remember this when that particular dessert from her childhood was placed on the table. And there, leaning up against the counter with plumes of cigarette smoke punctuating her quiet reserve, with questions on how we liked the food, was Beulah Graham Teal. Foot tapping, cheekbones looking sharp enough to cut your fingers on, and a way about her it took me several years to understand.

This was the look of a woman who was certain she had met your needs. This was the look of a woman who knew she had exceeded your expectations. She never sat at the table with us while we ate. I don't think I ever saw her eat the food she cooked. My mom is the same way—never eating with us after she makes dinner—but this felt different than the relief and retreat that would follow my mom making a meal. This was a victory cigarette enjoyed over the praise evident in clean plates that begged for seconds. This was satisfaction. But from what? Later, when I thought of this scenario, one of many that took shape over the course of our trips to see her, I realized it was self-satisfaction that dripped from the proud way she leaned against the counter, watching us eat the food she knew we could not resist.

But the backdrop to this calm was something I never got to see. Every ounce of the rage she had about potential never realized, about opportunities stolen from her simply because she was a black woman in the Jim Crow South, about the choices made for her that attempted to stifle her fire. I imagined her letting go of it all for the short while she spent cooking for her family, reconciled or defeated as she surged and stormed in the kitchen. But she'd never let you see the whipping winds or the rain of tears. Just the sunset aftermath—a bit of her triumph on full display, because, despite the facts of her life, my grandmother never saw herself as a victim. You weren't ever going to get to see the part of her that did battle, but you'd sure get to reap the rewards of it. And her reward—the fully possessed self-knowledge that her rage could be the cause of such sublime delight.

BLOODY BUTCHER
CORNBREAD

From Bianca Borges

2 cups Bloody Butcher cornmeal or other good-quality medium-coarse cornmeal

1½ cups (180 grams) all-purpose flour (or half all-purpose, half bread flour)

2 tablespoons sugar

1½ tablespoons baking powder

1¼ teaspoons kosher salt

¼ teaspoon baking soda

1¼ cups whole milk, at room temperature

¾ cup sour cream, at room temperature

2 large eggs, at room temperature

1 teaspoon vegetable oil, or 2 teaspoons lard

7 tablespoons unsalted butter, melted, plus 1 teaspoon for buttering

"I like cornbread moist, but not too crumbly," says Bianca, who grew up in Alabama and is now part of the team at Milk Street. "So I usually add a portion of bread flour for a firmer texture, just like my mom's bread, which is the best cornmeal I will ever eat. My mother's hand was sure and steady in the kitchen, despite confounding contradictions in other areas of life. Like most kitchen daughters of kitchen moms, I take the best of what I can remember and incorporate my own hand to create something good for this modern day."

"Bloody Butcher" is a darn good metaphor for all sorts of things, whatever floats your raging boat. It refers to the name of an heirloom dent corn variety with deep red kernels, an American soil crop since the 1800s. When ground into cornmeal, the color is a subtle purplish red, and the taste is deeply nutty and earthy. Bloody Butcher cornmeal can be found from several online sources (see Mail-Order Rage on page 163) or at farmers' markets; it's well worth seeking out. But this buttery cornbread can just as easily be made using any variety of good medium-coarse cornmeal. We love this with honey butter (see page 42) or drizzled with maple syrup.

Put a 10-inch cast-iron or stainless-steel skillet on the center rack and preheat the oven to 400°F.

Whisk together the cornmeal, flour, sugar, baking powder, salt, and baking soda, in a large bowl. Whisk together the milk, sour cream, and eggs until smooth, in another bowl.

Once the oven reaches temperature, *carefully* remove the hot skillet and add the oil and the 1 teaspoon butter. Tilt the skillet to coat the bottom and part way up the sides. Return the skillet to the oven while you mix the batter.

Add the milk mixture and the melted butter to the flour mixture and gently stir/fold until just combined, take care not to overmix. Carefully remove the hot skillet from the oven and pour the batter into the skillet. Bake until the top feels firm when lightly pressed, 20 to 25 minutes. Let cool in the skillet for at least 15 minutes before cutting. Serve hot, warm, or at room temperature. Store leftover cornbread, well wrapped, in the refrigerator for 1 day or in the freezer for up to 1 month; toast leftovers before serving.

SPICED BULGUR FLATBREADS (NANE SAUER)

From Naomi Duguid

2 cups *fine* bulgur

¼ teaspoon ground cumin

¼ teaspoon ground nigella seeds

⅛ teaspoon ground fenugreek

½ cup minced onion (about 1 small)

1½ teaspoons kosher salt, plus more for sprinkling

2 to 2¼ cups boiling water

About 1½ to 2 cups (180 to 240 grams) all-purpose or whole wheat flour, plus more for dusting

About ½ stick unsalted butter, melted, for brushing (optional)

"When I think about all the women around the world I've spent time with who bake daily or weekly for their families or as local bakers, it's humbling and also encouraging," says cookbook author and writer Naomi Duguid. "There's a fellowship of home bakers. I find myself thinking about them whenever I knead dough. I love kneading, for I can settle into the rhythms of it, feel the dough change under my hands, feel my muscles, and enjoy the memories and reflections that kneading triggers.

"I often think of the Kurdish women I met when I was in Iraqi Kurdistan. In Sulaymaniyah I learned a spiced version of a classic Kurdish bulgur flatbread. It's flavored with minced onion and a blend of ground cumin, nigella, and fenugreek. The breads are easy to make, flexible in their timing, and aromatic as they bake."

Bulgur flatbreads are delicious on their own, and can be served as a breakfast bread, as part of a mezze platter, or with cheese at the end of a meal. These are slightly smaller than the traditional breads, so they are easier to handle and have a wonderful nutty, dense, chewy texture.

Combine the bulgur, cumin, nigella, fenugreek, onion, and salt in a large bowl. Pour 1½ to 2 cups of the boiling water over the bulgur and stir to combine. Cover and set aside for 30 minutes.

Add 1½ cups of the flour to the bulgur mixture and start mixing the dough with your hands, squeezing it through your fingers to blend it. As you press and work it, the bulgur, softened by the hot water, will start to get sticky and, together with the flour, will form a dough. If your bulgur is very finely ground, you may be able to get by with adding only 1½ cups of flour, but I have found that with not-well-ground bulgur, I need to add a full 2 cups of flour and knead it thoroughly and firmly so that it comes together into a dough. If the dough feels dry, add the remaining ¼ cup water. (Bulgurs and flours vary, and the important thing is to have a moist, firm, kneadable dough.)

Cover the dough and set aside to rest for at least 1 hour or up to 3 hours. (If you wish to make only some of the dough into bread, and to keep the rest for the next day, cover and refrigerate. Bring back to room temperature before rolling out and baking.)

Half an hour before you plan to bake the flatbreads, position a rack in the upper third of the oven and preheat the oven to 450°F. Place a baking stone or unglazed quarry tiles on the upper rack to preheat.

Turn the dough out onto a lightly floured surface, pull it together into a block and then cut it into 12 equal pieces (first cut it into 4 equal pieces, then cut each of those pieces into thirds). Using your floured palms, flatten each piece into a disk. Turn the disk over and use your palm to flatten it into a roughly 5-inch round. Smooth the edges where necessary to tidy them up. Repeat to form two more rounds, then place them on a piece of parchment paper and use a flour-dusted wooden peel or the back of a baking sheet to transfer them onto the hot stone or tiles. (The parchment helps them slip right off the peel or baking sheet. If your oven will fit more than three at a time, feel free to bake them in larger batches.)

Bake for about 5 minutes, then use a long-handled spatula to turn the flatbreads over and bake for about 5 minutes more, until slightly touched with color and a little firmed up. Shape the remaining dough as the first flatbreads bake. Transfer the cooked flatbreads to a clean kitchen towel to keep warm. Brush each flatbread with a little melted butter, if you wish, and sprinkle with salt. Repeat with the remaining dough.

These are best eaten immediately.

POWER MUFFS

From Elizabeth Falkner

Cooking spray or butter,
for buttering (optional)

¾ cup loosely packed dark brown
or muscovado sugar

½ cup vegetable oil

1 large egg

2 tablespoons pure maple syrup

1½ cups toasted or
raw sunflower seeds

½ cup golden flaxseed meal

⅓ cup wheat germ

½ cup granola

¼ cup coarsely chopped walnuts

2 tablespoons chia seeds

2 tablespoons sesame seeds

1 teaspoon ground cinnamon

½ teaspoon freshly grated nutmeg

1 teaspoon baking powder

¼ teaspoon baking soda

1 teaspoon kosher salt

½ cup buttermilk

1 small apple, cored and cut into
½-inch cubes (about 1¼ cups)

½ cup goji berries, rehydrated in
water, well strained, and patted dry

"These muff(in)s are so packed with antioxidants and good-for-you nuts and seeds that you'll feel your superwoman powers with a vengeance," says Elizabeth Falkner, a creative artist, talented chef, and president of WCR (Women Chefs & Restaurateurs). *"Many of the things I cook and bake are often meant to fight the powers that be. I hate the notion that girls make pastry—and obviously we do—but we kick ass doing so!"* This recipe has a number of ingredients all available at health food stores. These muff(in)s are gluten-free and super easy, keep for several days (they also freeze beautifully), and are a perfect fortification for a march or marathon.

Position a rack in the center of the oven and preheat the oven to 325°F. Line a 12-cup muffin tin with paper liners or mist the cups with cooking spray.

Whisk the brown sugar, oil, egg, and maple syrup in a large bowl. Add the sunflower seeds, flaxseed meal, wheat germ, granola, walnuts, chia seeds, sesame seeds, cinnamon, and nutmeg and mix with a wooden spoon to combine evenly. Add the baking powder, baking soda, and salt and mix to combine evenly. Stir in the buttermilk, apple, and goji berries. Let the batter rest for 10 minutes.

Scoop the batter into the prepared tin, filling each cup just shy of the top. Bake until a toothpick inserted into the center of a muffin comes out clean, 25 to 30 minutes. Let cool in the tin for 5 minutes, then transfer the muffins to a wire rack and let cool to room temperature.

FROM

GOOD AND MAD

By REBECCA TRAISTER

At all the marches, all the rallies, you'll see one sign over and over again. It is a Mexican proverb, apparently taken from the Greek: "They thought they could bury us; they didn't know we were seeds." Women's anger has been buried, over and over again. But it has seeded the ground; we are the green shoots of furies covered up long ago.

If you happen to be reading this in the future, having stumbled across it in an attempt to find out if you're allowed to be angry about whatever you're angry about, let me say: yes. Yes you are allowed. You are in fact compelled.

And if you're reading this now, in its moment, with me; if you've gotten to this page because you've been feeling rage at the unfairness and injustice and at the flaws of this country and because your anger is making you want to change your life in order to change the world, then I have something incredibly important to say: Don't forget how this feels.

Tell a friend, write it down, explain it to your children now, so they will remember. And don't let anyone persuade you it wasn't right, or it was weird, or it was some quirky stage in your life when you went all political—*remember that, honey, that year you went crazy*? No. No. Don't let it ever become that. Because people will try.

The future will come, we hope. If we survive this, if we make it better—even just a little bit better, but I hope a lot better—the urgency will fade, perhaps the ire will subside, the relief will take you, briefly. And that's good, that's okay.

But then the world will come and tell you that you shouldn't get mad again, because you were kind of nuts and you never cooked dinner and you yelled at the TV and weren't so pretty and life will be easier when you get fun again. And it will be awfully tempting to put away the pictures of yourself in your pussy hat, to stuff your protest signs in the attic, and to slink back, away from the raw bite of fury, to ease back into whatever new reality is made after whatever advances we achieve now.

But I say to all the women reading this now, and to my future self: What you're angry about now—injustice—will still exist, even if you yourself are not experiencing it, or are tempted to stop thinking about *how* you experience it, and how you contribute to it. Others are still experiencing it, still mad; some of them are mad at you. Don't forget them; don't write off their anger. Stay mad for them. Stay mad *with* them. They're right to be mad and you're right to be mad alongside them.

Being mad is correct; being mad is American; being mad can be joyful and productive and connective. Don't *ever* let them talk you out of being mad again.

ZUCCHINI-ALMOND BREAD

From Rebecca Traister

Cooking spray

1 cup almonds

3 cups (360 grams) all-purpose flour

2 teaspoons baking powder

1¼ teaspoons fine salt

1 teaspoon baking soda

1 teaspoon ground cinnamon

3 large eggs

2 cups sugar

1 cup vegetable oil,
plus more if needed

2 cups grated zucchini
(about 1 large)

1 teaspoon pure almond extract
or vanilla extract

Rebecca Traister, author of Good and Mad, *provided so much inspiration for this project. We were so thrilled when she shared her recipe for this moist zucchini bread. It's got the right note of cinnamon and has great texture—thanks to ground almonds. You can add other nuts or flavorings; Traister recommends ground walnuts and vanilla, or ground pecans and anise. It's the ultimate breakfast bread or pick-me-up snack, served with strong hot coffee or iced tea.*

Position a rack in the center of the oven and preheat the oven to 350°F. Mist a 9 x 5-inch loaf pan with cooking spray or brush with oil.

Grind the almonds in a blender or food processor until *almost* finely ground.

Whisk together the flour, baking powder, salt, baking soda, and cinnamon, in a medium bowl.

In a stand mixer fitted with the paddle attachment, combine the eggs, sugar, and oil and beat on medium speed until slightly thickened, about 3 minutes. With the mixer on low speed, slowly add the flour mixture and beat until fully incorporated. Add the zucchini, ground almonds, and almond extract and mix until the batter is smooth.

Transfer the batter to the prepared pan. Bake until golden brown and a toothpick inserted into the center of the bread comes out clean, about 1 hour 15 minutes. Let cool in the pan for 5 to 10 minutes, then turn the bread out of the pan and serve warm or at room temperature. Wrap tightly in foil and store at room temperature for up to 4 days.

SPICED GRANOLA
with APRICOTS AND CARDAMOM

From Mindy Fox

3 cups rolled oats, preferably extra-thick

1 cup pecans or walnuts, coarsely chopped

1 cup unsalted hulled raw pepitas (pumpkin seeds)

½ cup sesame seeds

½ cup uncooked white quinoa

½ cup plus 1 tablespoon pure maple syrup

½ cup virgin (unrefined) coconut oil

1½ teaspoons kosher salt

1 teaspoon pure vanilla extract

1 teaspoon ground cardamom

½ teaspoon freshly ground black pepper or cayenne pepper, or a mix

¾ cup dried apricots, coarsely chopped

"I started making granola when I was nineteen years old," food writer Mindy Fox explains. "I was a sophomore at the University of Wisconsin-Madison, also known as the 'Berkeley of the Midwest.' Political activism was a way of life with jam-packed rallies and marches. It was there that I found community and my political voice.

"Cardamom tilts this granola into new territory, and ground black pepper (or cayenne) warms up the spice. The nuts and seeds can be varied according to whatever is available in your larder when the granola-making mood strikes. Almonds can be used in place of pecans or walnuts; sunflower seeds can be swapped in for pepitas and flaxseed or hemp seed for the crunchy quinoa; or you can use a mix of any or all of the above."

Serve with milk or yogurt, with citrus segments or berries, as a snack, or over scoops of vanilla ice cream for dessert.

Position a rack in the center of the oven and preheat the oven to 325°F. Line an 18 x 13-inch rimmed baking sheet with parchment paper.

Combine the oats, nuts, pepitas, sesame seeds, and quinoa, in a large bowl.

In a small saucepan, combine the maple syrup, oil, salt, vanilla, cardamom, and pepper. Heat over medium-low heat, whisking occasionally, until the oil has melted and the mixture is just warmed through (do not bring it to a simmer).

Pour the maple mixture over the nut mixture, scraping every last drop out of the pan with a rubber spatula. Stir well to combine, then spread the mixture in an even layer over the prepared baking sheet. Bake, stirring once halfway through, until the granola is lightly golden, 35 to 40 minutes (it will still be damp; this is okay). Stir in the apricots, then bake for 5 minutes more.

Transfer the baking sheet to a wire rack and let the granola cool completely (it will dry and firm up as it cools), then break up any large clumps, if you wish, and transfer to an airtight container. The granola can be stored at room temperature for up to 2 weeks.

BETTER BREAD

*T*here are few things more beautiful than the seductive scent of a freshly baked quick bread or slow-rising bread. But for some reason, baking yeast bread scares otherwise sane cooks. We have found that these simple tips help calm and provide the confidence bakers need to produce great bread.

QUICK BREADS rely on baking powder and baking soda for their lift; always make sure your leaveners are fresh and potent (see page xix).

HAVING A LIGHT TOUCH when mixing the batter or dough for biscuits, cornbread, or muffins results in more tender and delicate results. Be careful not to overmix, combine until just moistened—a few lumps are okay.

SOME YEAST BREAD RECIPES call for bread flour because it contains more protein than other types of flours. Protein, when moistened and then mixed and kneaded, turns to gluten, which is exactly what you want for the structure of bread. Bread flour is ideal for making breads with a crisp and chewy crust.

TO LEARN MORE ABOUT YEAST, see page xxii.

DON'T UNDERESTIMATE THE POWER OF SALT in bread dough. Salt has several chemical interactions, when mixed with flour and yeast, that are crucial to good bread.

STAND MIXERS (see page xxiv) aren't cheap but can be so helpful when mixing dough. When working with a stand mixer, you tend to need less flour than if you're working by hand. Mixers also help dough come together into an even, soft, pliable ball.

KNEADING CAN BE MEDITATIVE. You want to work the dough gently but with purpose and knead it long enough to develop the web of gluten. Stay focused on how soft and pliable the dough is, and read the directions to know exactly what you're looking for in terms of the dough's texture (a nicely kneaded dough is like a baby's bottom).

WORK ON A LIGHTLY FLOURED SURFACE. If you dust too heavily, your dough may pick up too much flour, and the resulting bread will be tough. That said, if it's a rainy day, you may need to add more flour while kneading; if you live in a dry climate, you might use less.

WHEN KNEADING, PRESS GENTLY TO ROLL THE DOUGH over the counter with the heel of your hands, give it a quarter turn, fold it in half, and repeat. If you see the dough tearing, it's a sign that you may be kneading too vigorously.

PATIENCE IS KEY when it comes to baking bread. Some recipes call for multiple risings, meaning there may be hours of waiting involved. Do not rush this. Letting dough rise for the specified amount of time (or until the desired volume is reached) is key to developing great-tasting and -textured breads.

BAKE AND WATCH! Once you finally put your bread in the oven, keep an eye on it through the oven window so you can see if it's baking too fast, browning too much (and you need to rotate the pan), etc.

TO TEST IF A BREAD IS FULLY BAKED, remove it from the pan, if needed turn it over, and tap on the bottom of the loaf; it should sound hollow. To take the guesswork out of it, use an instant-read thermometer; baked bread should register between 190° and 200°F.

ALWAYS LET YOUR BREAD COOL for at least 15 minutes before slicing. A serrated knife is best for slicing all types of breads.

COOL QUICK BREADS, MUFFINS, AND YEASTED BREADS completely before wrapping for storing. Don't store bread in the refrigerator; it will actually go stale faster. Freeze breads in reusable storage bags. If you think you won't eat a whole loaf at once, slice it before freezing. Do not thaw bread in the microwave; microwaving will dry it out. Instead, let it thaw at room temperature or in a 300°F oven.

MOST BREADS WILL KEEP IN A PAPER OR CLOTH BAG AT ROOM TEMPERATURE (with the exception of baguettes) for at least 2 days. Breads also freeze well; double wrap and place in a freezer bag, then freeze for up to 3 months.

CONFIDENCE AND PRACTICE = DELICIOUS BREAD.

Let Sit Until Doubled In Size. Wait, What?

You know the baking instructions that tell you to let the dough rise "until doubled in size," and you're like, "Wait, what? I can't even remember how big it was when I started!" Yup, we're with you. Here's a great little tip from Katherine: Place the dough in the bowl, cover with plastic or reusable wrap, and, using a marker, draw a circle on the wrap that is roughly the size of the dough. Inside the circle write the time you started letting the dough rise. And then . . . an hour or so later, you can see the original size of the dough and how much it has risen. Brillant? Yeah, we thought so.

TYPING IS A

Growing up in my family, women didn't channel rage in the kitchen. The sound of anger came through furtive clicks on the computer keyboard, multiple copies of a letter printed on the clunky inkjet, then placed into a large envelope, and handed off for shipping. Its recipients would be listed by name and title, their colleagues and sometimes board members carbon-copied—back when "cc" meant a person actually received a physical document with enclosures. My mother and my grandmother handled institutional upset, particularly in cases that threatened me, by writing clear, exacting letters to persons of import, sometimes together, one dictating turns of phrase to the other. My mother, the media person with the fast typing skills, my grandmother, retired, but still every bit the statewide public agency director she used to be, in cahoots in my defense.

This dance took place when I was in junior high in California. When a recruiter from an esteemed private high school on the East Coast assured my family that if I had a strong application and was accepted, I'd receive ample scholarship money. He lied. He was only trying to get his recruitment numbers up. I was indeed accepted to the school. Floating on the high of my eighth-grade student council presidency, I dreamed of following in the footsteps of world leaders. But the financial package was laughable, insulting even, given the promise. The dangled opportunity stung—I wouldn't have been granted permission to pursue the lengthy application process had my family understood the reality.

The letter writing took place throughout my parents' divorce and the ensuing custody issues that emerged, as judges let my father run amok with court filings. It included other incidents like when a white doctor from Stanford, my mom's alma mater, yelled at me over the phone. It was the late '90s and I'd called a number listed on the website of a university-sponsored summer science program geared toward precollegiate black high school students. I still don't know what I did to make the doctor blow his lid. But when my mother observed my shrinking posture as I hung up the phone, she practically demanded a transcript of the brief phone exchange. Shortly after I recounted the conversation, they were at it again. Mom and Grandma at the screen and keys, questioning the professionalism of a white doctor darn near cursing out a teenager—who he probably figured was an "underprivileged" student not worthy of pulling him off his rounds with

KIND OF FURY

By **OSAYI ENDOLYN**

a casual inquiry. It wasn't my fault the number was on the website or that the nurse didn't take a message. I had simply asked for the guy in charge. Mom sent a letter to the appropriate university brass and copied then provost Condoleezza Rice. I'm fairly certain she signed her name with her graduation year and master's degree program—journalism.

In these instances I understood that sometimes people at big institutions didn't expect much from me, my mother, and my grandmother. I understood that writing a thing down could have a different type of impact for me as black girl, as the descendant of black women. I understood that asking certain questions to specific people at a particular time, in print, could do a thing called putting folks "on notice."

My mother's choice to document a grievance of her middle-school-aged child getting caught up in a mash of private boarding school applicant quotas might not have changed a longstanding and imperfect system. But it showed me that you don't have to sit with how acts of systemic aggression make you feel. Sometimes you can make the responsible party confront the mess they made. On the matter of the Stanford science program, I recall that my mother received a letter of forthright apology from a dean, who acknowledged that the doctor's behavior was wrong. Reading between the lines of bureaucratic speak, she was satisfied with the response. My mother had clocked the underlying racism in a white doctor-gatekeeper, recruiting bright, young black students, only to shame such students when they asked to be heard.

She didn't allow me to apply to the camp. "I'm not sending you up there," she said with a "humph." I thought for some time that she'd backed me into a corner of a missed opportunity, that she'd gotten caught up in indignation. Now I understand her decision. My mom was teaching me a different type of power, one that I recognize in my own writing and actions—the **power of choice**. I see it now in my private emails to editors about racist publishing decisions and in customer service letters that confront employee bias and certainly in my editorial work. *I won't always be able to stop American systems from treating you like you don't belong*, my mom was implying. But Mom and Grandma showed me that choosing not just when to opt in, but how to opt out, could say just as much, if not more.

THEPLA *and* CHUNDO (MANGO CHUTNEY)

From Preeti Mistry

1 cup fresh or frozen fenugreek leaves, coarsely chopped

1 tablespoon finely minced garlic (about 3 medium cloves)

1 tablespoon finely minced peeled ginger

1 tablespoon minced serrano chile (with seeds if you like it HOT)

½ cup plain whole-milk yogurt

1 teaspoon ground turmeric

2 teaspoons kosher salt

1 cup (120 grams) whole wheat flour

1 cup (120 grams) all-purpose flour, plus ¼ cup (30 grams) for dusting

About ¼ cup vegetable oil

About ½ cup warm water (110°F)

Chundo (recipe follows), for serving

Indian cookbook author and activist Preeti Mistry says she "loves the repetitive meditation of cooking, and especially working with dough. When you first start rolling any sort of Indian flatbread, the process is not at all meditative. It requires focus to teach your hands and mind to work together with the thin rolling pin (called a belan) and the dough. To keep each piece even and round is at first a struggle. Growing up, my mother and aunts would use a phrase to describe a young woman who had practiced long enough to start to 'get it'; translated into English, it literally means 'her hands have sat down.' It's the moment where the struggle gives way and your mind starts to drift, but each paratha (flatbread) still comes out perfect. In the industry we call it 'muscle memory.' I prefer saying my hands have sat down."

Thepla, one of Preeti's favorite Gujarati flatbreads, are traditionally made for taking on a journey or traveling. If you can't find fresh fenugreek leaves (also called methi) you can use frozen ones, which are available in most Indian grocery stores and online (see Mail-Order Rage on page 163). Thepla are great dipped into chundo (an unripe mango chutney) and plain yogurt, or just eaten plain.

Mix the fenugreek, garlic, ginger, chile, and yogurt together in a medium-large bowl.

Sprinkle the turmeric and salt over the yogurt mixture and mix with a wooden spoon. Add the whole wheat and all-purpose flours and 1 teaspoon of the oil and stir to combine. Slowly add the water a few tablespoons at a time, until the dough starts to come together, then use your hands to knead the dough, adding more water as needed to make the dough soft and pliable. (If the dough gets too wet, add a dusting of flour.) Form the dough into a ball. Cover the bowl and let rest for 30 minutes.

Put the remaining oil into a small bowl and set it near the stove, with a pastry brush alongside. Divide the dough into 12 equal pieces and roll each piece into a ball. On a lightly floured surface, use a (preferably) thin rolling pin, like a dowel or a tapered French rolling pin to roll each ball into a disk about ⅛ inch thick and 4 inches wide. (If

continued

you are using a rolling pin with handles, use a light touch.) If the dough is sticking to the work surface, run a bench scraper under it to release it. Meanwhile, heat a medium cast-iron or nonstick skillet over medium heat.

Add about ¾ teaspoon of the oil to the pan, then lay a disk of dough in the pan and cook until browned on both sides, about a minute per side. Transfer the flatbread to a paper towel–lined plate. Repeat with the remaining dough, adding additional oil as needed. Serve warm or at room temperature, with chundo for dipping.

CHUNDO
(MANGO CHUTNEY)

MAKES ABOUT 2 CUPS

2 large unripe mangoes

1½ cups sugar

2 teaspoons Kashmiri red chili powder, or 1½ teaspoons paprika and ½ teaspoon cayenne pepper, or to taste

3 whole cloves

1 teaspoon cumin seeds

Peel the mangoes and grate the flesh on the largest holes of a box grater. Discard the pits.

In a medium saucepan, combine the mango, sugar, and chili powder.

In a small dry skillet, toast the cloves and cumin seeds over low heat until they just begin to smoke, then stir them into the mango mixture. Cook over medium-low heat until the sugar has dissolved or the mixture bubbles. Reduce the heat to low and cook, stirring frequently as the mixture thickens, about 15 minutes. Let cool, then store in a jar or other airtight container in the refrigerator for up to 1 week.

CHALLAH

From Darra Goldstein

3 large eggs

2 (¼-ounce) packets rapid-rise yeast
(4½ teaspoons total)

2 cups warm water (110°F)

4 teaspoons fine salt

½ cup sugar

1¼ cups vegetable oil,
plus more for buttering

7 cups (840 grams) all-purpose flour,
plus more for dusting

Poppy or sesame seeds (optional)

"Long before the rise of #procrastibaking, or even hashtags, I baked my way through grad school. It was a way of connecting to the tangible world, a necessary escape from the world of books, allowing me to banish the cerebral and revel in the sensual, if only for a little while," writes cookbook author, professor, and leading authority on Russian cooking Darra Goldstein. When we asked for a favorite recipe, she immediately offered us this challah: *"Dough was my favored medium, since I could get my hands into it, and challah soon became my go-to recipe. I could play with the strands of dough, making simple braids if I was short on time or creating more elaborate loaves with multiple twists and turns. The more often I baked challah, the more I realized that it also connected me with my Jewish heritage, the centuries-old community of women who baked these loaves ritually each week for the Sabbath. Though I'm not religious, I shared in that sisterhood.*

"This challah recipe contains seven ingredients, representing the seven days of the week. But I don't always wait till Friday to bake it, and even when I do, I often can't wait till the loaves cool to break into this rich bread. If, like me, you enjoy challah's beautiful long fibers, be sure to tear the loaves rather than slicing them."

Three loaves of challah may seem like a lot, but if you're putting in the effort, it's great to have a lot to show for it! These freeze beautifully, and leftover challah is great for French toast.

Beat the eggs in a small bowl with a fork, then transfer 2 tablespoons to a separate small bowl and set aside to use as an egg wash.

Whisk together the yeast and ¼ cup of the warm water in a large bowl, then set aside until bubbling, about 10 minutes.

Add the remaining 1¾ cups warm water, the salt, sugar, oil, eggs, and 3 cups (320 grams) of the flour and stir together with a wooden spoon to make a wet dough. Beat in the remaining 4 cups (520 grams) flour to make a shaggy dough. Turn the dough out onto a lightly floured work surface and knead by hand until pliable and shiny, 8 to 10 minutes. Form the dough into a ball. (Alternatively, prepare the dough in a stand mixer fitted with the dough hook, stopping to scrape down the sides of the bowl as needed, then knead the dough on medium speed until pliable and shiny, about 5 minutes.)

Brush a large bowl with a little oil and place the dough in the bowl, turning it once to oil the top. Cover with plastic or reusable wrap and let rise in a warm place until doubled in size (see page 57), 45 minutes to 1 hour 30 minutes, depending on how warm the room is.

Preheat the oven to 350°F. Brush two baking sheets lightly with oil.

Punch down the dough and turn it out onto a clean work surface. Divide it into 3 equal pieces (about 560 grams each). Divide one piece into thirds (about 190 grams each), then roll and stretch each portion into a rope about 12 inches long. Braid the ropes together, pinching the ends together at the top and bottom and turning them under to seal. Repeat with the remaining dough. You will have three braided loaves. Carefully transfer the loaves to the prepared pans. Cover with clean kitchen towels and let rise once more until puffy, 20 to 45 minutes, depending on the room's temperature.

Gently brush the loaves with the egg wash and sprinkle with poppy seeds, if desired. Bake for 40 to 45 minutes, until the loaves are nicely browned and sound hollow when tapped on the bottom. Transfer to a wire rack to cool.

RIGHTEOUS BABES, **ANGER,** AND FINDING HUMILITY

A CONVERSATION WITH ANI DIFRANCO

Ani DiFranco is a Grammy Award–winning singer, songwriter, poet, feminist, and activist, and the author of the memoir No Walls and the Recurring Dream. *She has released more than twenty albums, started her own record label, Righteous Babe Records, and is a mother of two.*

KATHY GUNST: Does the word "rage" resonate with you?

ANI DIFRANCO: Yeah, absolutely. I mean, I don't know if you've heard, but I've been known as an angry woman for a long time.

KATHY: Yeah, I've heard.

ANI: There is a lot of justifiable rage in this world but, for some reason, I've had my rage portrayed as, well, not a rational response to things. I guess if you mean I'm a woke woman or a woman being present in society, then okay, I'll take "angry" as my mantle, but that never feels like what they're saying. It's like my rage becomes this thing they can reduce me to in order to push me off to the side, like I have some kind of extremist take on

things. I mean, what other than rage is the appropriate response to the Kavanaugh hearing?

KATHY: I've been going back and listening to your repertoire of songs, and in "Not a Pretty Girl," you write:

> *I am not an angry girl*
>
> *but it seems like I've got everyone fooled*
>
> *every time I say something they find hard to hear*
>
> *they chalk it up to my anger,*
>
> *never to their own fear*

ANI: I guess that's exactly what we're talking about here, isn't it? What happens when you bring up the inconvenient truths of society. It's funny to say for a majority population, but females are a marginalized group. You will be portrayed as a shrill, irrational person and it's hard to hold on to that core truth inside yourself, to have faith in the validity of your own outrage.

KATHY: You are a parent now. How does that change the way you express yourself and see the world?

ANI: The moment you bring kids into the world, you pressure yourself to move through the rage into other responses in order to teach your children. My daughter, for instance, I want to teach her to find peace with it all. Not be constricted with rage her whole life. You instinctually are trying to teach them how to deal with their rage, achieve inner peace, even in a very fucked-up society.

KATHY: Do you feel you need to tamp things down?

ANI: The only way you can teach is by achieving it. Employ more humility, more wisdom, more acceptance. Strange words because, of course, you have to keep voting for justice and equality. But you don't want your daughters to be overwhelmed by their feminist outrage and get stuck in it. You [the parent] have to get unstuck to show them what balance looks like. I look at the anger response as a luxury I can't afford in this culture of infinite outrage.

KATHY: Isn't your music your way of moving through it?

ANI: Oh, definitely.

KATHY: I was watching old videos of you playing guitar, and it was almost aggressive, the way you played the instrument. How has your relationship to your music shifted over the years?

ANI: When I look back at my early '90s songs, I'm like, "Whoa. There is a girl just expending a lot of energy toward survival, the daily task of self-preservation." I was trying to elbow out space for myself and also to empower myself so I'm not always the victim on the run. I feel like decades of writing myself into being has worked. I do feel, when I listen to my old songs, that I'm in a different place now, a safer place, a stronger place, a place that's my own that I made.

KATHY: What advice would you give young women these days in thinking about our threat to reproductive rights, the president, the government? What do you tell a young (or older) woman who is losing hope?

ANI: It's easy to look around and think, *This is the way it is*. But if you look back ten minutes behind you, that's not the way it is. And so it can be true about the way you move forward. Political involvement on the part of women is essential. Starting with our participation at the ballot box. The right to vote was hard fought for, for so many of us in this country, and it's a shame to squander it. Voter suppression is a tactic so fiercely and widely used precisely because our vote gives us so much power. When I step up to vote, it's like a spiritual act for me, it's an act of faith. Faith in democracy, faith in humankind. Of course, women need not only vote, but to then be sitting at the table when we're designing society. Women should hold half of public offices.

KATHY: Speaking of the table, is cooking or being in the kitchen ever a place of refuge for you?

ANI: Cooking is something of an art. It's like the piano. I wish I had taken lessons. It's like a language I can say "please" and "thank you" in, but I know there's so much more to express.

KATHY: Yeah, going into the kitchen and baking doesn't solve the problems of the world, but it does offer something of a balm, a refuge. A place to regroup before you go back out to fight the good fight.

ANI: It's like the most empowering stance to take. It's a way of saying, "I am not going to let my whole body, mind, and soul be overwhelmed and sabotaged by you today. I'm going to put smiles on my face and my kids' faces and we're going to be joyful today despite you."

WHEN I STEP UP TO VOTE, IT'S LIKE A SPIRITUAL ACT FOR ME, **IT'S AN ACT OF FAITH.**

MAPLE WALNUT
PULL-APART BREAD

From Katherine Alford

For the Dough

3 cups (360 grams) all-purpose flour, plus more for dusting

¾ cup whole milk

¼ cup plus 2 tablespoons water

1 (¼-ounce) packet rapid-rise yeast (2¼ teaspoons)

6 tablespoons unsalted butter, melted, plus room-temperature butter for buttering

⅓ cup granulated sugar

1 large egg, at room temperature, beaten

1½ teaspoons pure vanilla extract

½ teaspoon fine salt

To Assemble

3 tablespoons unsalted butter, melted, plus room-temperature butter for buttering

2 tablespoons pure maple syrup

About 1⅓ cups walnuts, finely chopped

I was obsessed with the notion of a pull-apart bread. What better metaphor for my growing rage as the patriarchy works overtime to repress the rights of anyone who is not a white, straight, cisgender man? I want to pull apart systems that put children in detention, don't believe Black Lives Matter, deny transgender equality, are dulled to school shootings, objectify women, negate climate change, and reward grifters and liars with the highest offices in the land.

I went a little insane developing this recipe. I made spreadsheets, watched videos, tested and retested. Kathy threatened an intervention, but I was determined to crack the code on this sweet bread. In the end it was worth it, the results were both delicious and comforting. It's just a bread, and it won't change the world, but it reminded me that when we don't lose heart and stay true to the hard work, change will come.

Make the dough: In a medium saucepan, whisk together ¼ cup (30 grams) of the flour, ¼ cup of the milk, and the ¼ cup water until smooth. Heat over medium heat, whisking continuously, until thick and smooth, 2 to 3 minutes. Transfer the mixture to the bowl of a stand mixer and, by hand, whisk in the remaining ½ cup milk, the 2 tablespoons water, the yeast, melted butter, granulated sugar, egg, and vanilla until smooth. Attach the dough hook, add the remaining 2¾ cups (330 grams) flour and the salt and knead on medium-low speed until smooth, about 10 minutes. (It can take a couple of minutes for all the flour to become drawn into the dough—it's okay to turn off the machine and scoot the flour in toward the dough hook.) Don't be concerned if the dough looks slightly wet.

Turn the dough out onto a clean work surface, lightly dust with flour, and form into a ball. Lightly butter a medium bowl. Place the dough in the bowl and cover with plastic or reusable wrap. Let rise in a warm place until doubled in size (see page 57), light, and puffy, about 1 hour, depending on how warm the room is.

Assemble the bread: Brush an 8- or 9½-inch Bundt pan with room-temperature butter.

continued

MAPLE WALNUT PULL-APART BREAD

(continued)

For the Glaze

½ cup confectioners' sugar

2 tablespoons pure maple syrup

¼ teaspoon pure maple extract
(or pure vanilla extract)

About 2 teaspoons whole milk

Turn the dough out onto your work surface and lightly stretch it into an 18 x 4-inch rectangle. (Take care not to overwork the dough, or the final bread may be tough.) Divide the rectangle in half lengthwise and then cut both halves into 1½- to 2-inch pieces; you should have 18 to 20 pieces. (A pizza wheel makes quick work of this.) Tuck the edges of each piece under and gently roll into a ball, placing them on a sheet of parchment paper on your work surface as you go. Brush them evenly with the melted butter, then brush with the maple syrup. Put the walnuts on a plate and roll each ball in the nuts to coat. Arrange the balls in the prepared pan in two layers. (At this point, if you'd like to serve the bread for breakfast or brunch, you can cover the pan and refrigerate the dough overnight. Bring it to room temperature and let rise in a warm place until the dough is puffy and fills the pan, about 1 hour, then bake as instructed.)

Cover the pan with a clean kitchen towel and let rise in a warm place until the dough is puffy and fills the pan, 1 hour to 1 hour 30 minutes, depending on how warm the room is.

Position a rack in the center of the oven and preheat the oven to 350°F.

Cover the pan loosely with a piece of aluminum foil and bake for 25 minutes, then remove the foil and bake until golden brown or an instant-read thermometer inserted into the bread registers 190° to 200°F, 10 to 15 minutes more. Let cool in the pan for 10 minutes, then turn the bread out onto a wire rack set over a piece of parchment paper to cool.

Meanwhile, make the glaze: In a small bowl, mix the confectioners' sugar, maple syrup, maple extract, and milk to make a thick but pourable glaze.

When cool, drizzle the glaze over the bread. Let the glaze set, about 10 minutes, then serve.

WE CAN BE SWEET & SAVORY

By KATHERINE ALFORD

In the food world, people are often divided into bakers and savory cooks; and all too often, these roles get gendered. Men get the knives and flame and women get the sugar and butter. Women make cookies and men become professional pastry chefs. I heard this repeatedly in the years I worked in professional kitchens. There was no shame in men saying they didn't feel comfortable with desserts. But if I did the inverse, like "I don't feel comfortable butchering, or grilling a steak, or working the hot line," I wouldn't be taken seriously. I had to be up for anything. I totally relate to the quote "Ginger Rogers did everything [Fred Astaire] did, backwards and in high heels."

In restaurants in the 1980s, it wasn't unusual to be the only woman on staff and to endure blatant and outrageous sexism. I was harrassed and shamed, and had to tolerate mansplaining that would make your head explode. (My favorite: "You know you can't whip egg whites when you have your period. It does something to the eggs." Who knew my uterus was so magical?) When a new chef was hired in the four-star restaurant that I worked in, I was offered the job of running the pastry and dessert department, not because I was any better than the highly skilled crew in place, but because I was "the girl." But in the long run, I was better off. I developed a wider range of skills that served me in my long career. I became a careful baker; I liked the science, the math, the discipline of baking, the satisfaction. I loved the nuance that goes into baking, the way the temperature of butter can make all the difference in a flaky pie crust, the way measuring improperly can throw off a cookie. And the big baking secret: Confidence is your most important ingredient. It's ironic that women get pushed into the part of cooking that requires the most math, chemistry, and precision. So, if you want your daughters to excel at STEM (science, technology, engineering, and math), bring them into the kitchen. Bake with them. The results will be sweet and empowering.

GRAPE AND ROSEMARY FOCACCIA

MAKES ONE 18 X 13-INCH FOCACCIA; SERVES 8 TO 10

From Katherine Alford

2 cups warm water (110°F)

3 tablespoons sugar

1 (¼-ounce) packet active dry yeast (2¼ teaspoons)

5 cups (600 grams) bread flour

9 tablespoons extra-virgin olive oil, plus more for greasing

1 tablespoon kosher salt, plus more or coarse sea salt for sprinkling

Cooking spray

1 pound red seedless grapes

2 teaspoons minced fresh rosemary leaves, plus sprigs for sprinkling

Freshly cracked black pepper

Focaccia is an alchemy of air, wheat, salt, extra-virgin olive oil—generous amounts of oil—and time. The best ones are made with a very wet dough, one that almost crosses the line into a batter. Because of that, a plastic pastry scraper is essential here. Use it to move the dough (instead of just using your hands), and it will be easier to handle. Make the dough the day before you plan to serve the focaccia; the slow rise makes for a lighter and more luscious bread. This version with red grapes is delicious served with cheese or salad, or as part of an antipasti with prosciutto and salami. Customize it with the addition of walnuts or cracked fennel seeds, swap out the grapes for roasted small tomatoes, or leave it plain with just coarse sea salt and herbs.

Pour ¼ cup of the warm water into a small bowl and add a generous pinch of the sugar. Sprinkle the yeast on the surface—don't stir. Set aside until creamy and bubbling, about 5 minutes.

In the bowl of a stand mixer, combine the remaining 1¾ cups warm water, remaining sugar, the flour, ¼ cup of the oil, and the salt and mix by hand with a wooden spoon to make a rough dough. Add the yeast mixture, attach the dough hook, and mix on medium-low speed for 10 minutes to make a soft, very slack dough that looks unmanageable but is not. (If needed, scrape down the sides of the bowl to combine.) The dough will be more like a wet batter.

Brush a large bowl with a little oil. Use a flexible pastry scraper or rubber spatula to transfer the dough to the bowl. Cover with plastic or reusable wrap or a clean kitchen towel and let rise in a warm place until the dough has doubled in size and large bubbles come to the surface, about 1 hour, depending on how warm the room is (see page 57).

Brush a 13 x 9-inch baking pan with 2 tablespoons of the oil. Turn the dough out into the pan. Using the pastry scraper, press the dough out into a rectangle. Slip the pastry scraper under the edges of the dough and fold it in thirds like a letter. Rotate the dough 90 degrees and repeat

continued

the letter fold. (This easy kneading builds structure and coats the layers with oil.) Mist a piece of plastic or reusable wrap with cooking spray or brush it lightly with oil and cover the dough. Refrigerate overnight or for up to 24 hours.

Drizzle an 18 x 13-inch baking sheet with 2 tablespoons of the oil. Transfer the cold dough to the baking sheet—again, the pastry scraper is your friend here. Cut a piece of parchment paper the size of the baking sheet and lightly brush it with oil or mist with cooking spray. Lay the oiled side of the parchment on top of the dough and press against the paper to stretch out the dough to fill the baking sheet. If the dough is resistant to stretching, wait for 10 minutes to allow it to relax, then try again. Remove the parchment. *The dough needs to be covered but not with anything on the surface; I use another inverted baking sheet.* Let the dough rise until it fills the baking sheet and gets very light and pillowy, 2 to 2 hours 30 minutes.

Meanwhile, position a rack in the lower third of the oven and preheat the oven to 425°F.

In a small oven-safe skillet or pan, toss the grapes with the remaining 1 tablespoon oil and season with salt. Roast until the grapes are juicy and slightly shriveled, about 10 minutes. Scatter the minced rosemary over the grapes and season generously with pepper. Let cool.

Uncover the dough and gently drop the grapes into it (I am a super nerd and use chopsticks for this, but it's fun to watch the grapes slip into the pillowy dough). Set aside until large air bubbles can be seen on the surface, about 20 minutes.

Scatter sea salt and rosemary sprigs over the dough. Bake until golden brown, about 30 minutes. Run an offset spatula under the focaccia to release it from the baking sheet, then slip it onto a wire rack to cool. Serve warm or at room temperature.

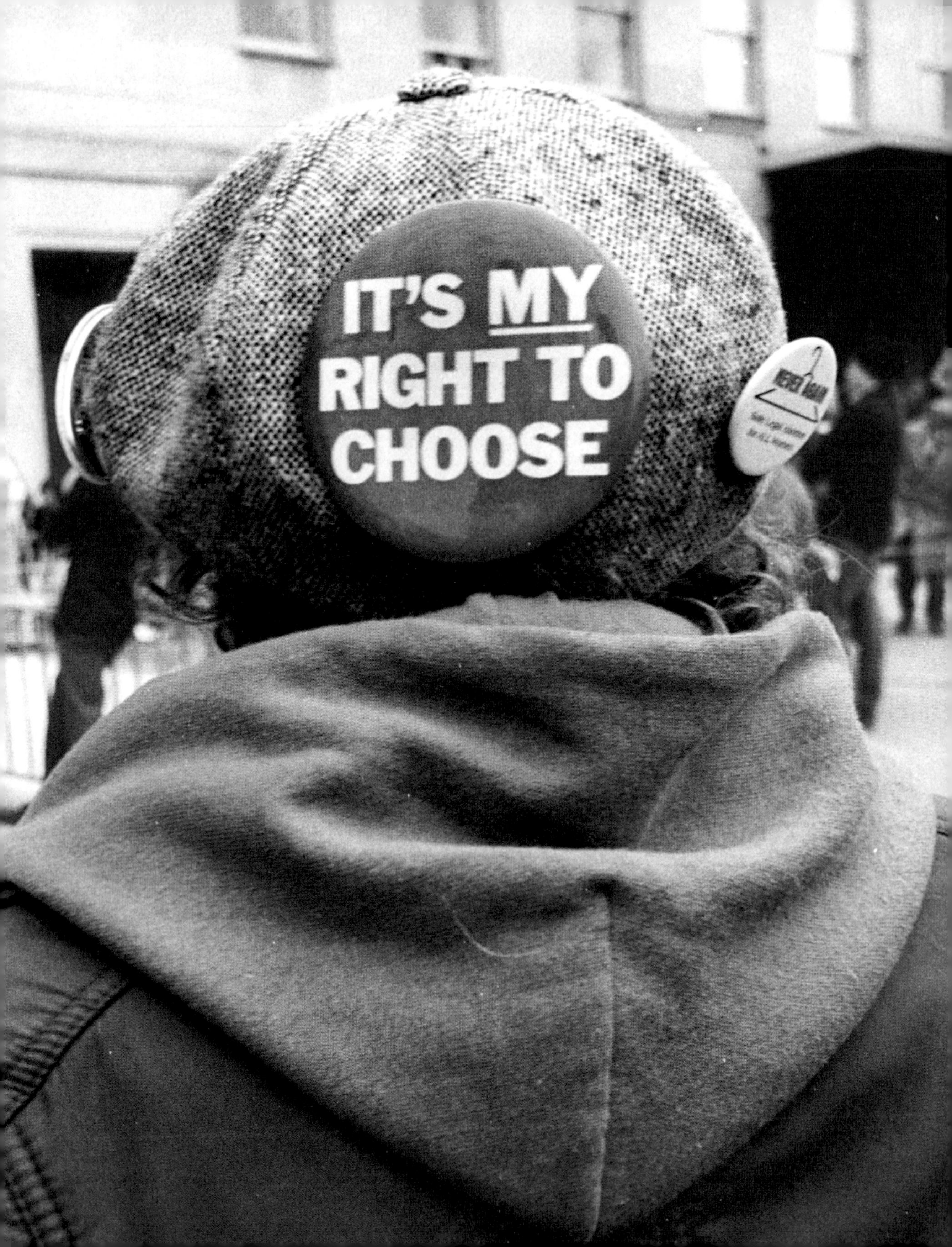
IT'S MY
RIGHT TO
CHOOSE

3

BAKE DOWN *the* PATRIARCHY:

CAKES

RECIPE LIST

BLUEBERRY BUTTERMILK BUCKLE

From Genevieve Ko

Cooking spray or butter,
for buttering the pan

1¾ cups (210 grams) all-purpose flour,
plus more for dusting

1 cup sugar

1 teaspoon baking powder

½ teaspoon baking soda

½ teaspoon fine salt

6 tablespoons salted butter, cut into
½-inch cubes and chilled

2 large eggs

1 teaspoon pure vanilla extract

¾ cup buttermilk

1¾ cups blueberries

"Fresh blueberries cause the top of this cake to buckle and caramelize into the batter while baking," explains Genevieve Ko, food writer and Los Angeles Times *cooking editor.* "They become nearly jammy pockets of berry-ness in the tender buttermilk vanilla cake. While you can add spices or other seasonings to the batter, this cake is all about simplicity—in its execution, taste, and texture. As much as I love fantastic layered creations or complex combinations, I sometimes crave a plain little cake with a cup of coffee. It's about all I can handle when juggling work and parenting. This cake is a great break from it all—it doesn't demand much of me, but gives plenty of pleasure."*

The batter for this light buttermilk cake is made entirely in a food processor, so it's impossible to screw up. Serve the cake dusted with confectioners' sugar or top it with crème fraîche, whipped cream, or vanilla ice cream.

Position a rack in the center of the oven and preheat the oven to 350°F. Coat an 8-inch square cake pan with cooking spray, or butter the pan and dust it with flour, then tap out any excess.

In a food processor, combine the flour, sugar, baking powder, baking soda, and salt and pulse until well mixed. Add the butter and pulse until coarse crumbs form, about 15 pulses. Add the eggs and vanilla and pulse until smooth, stopping to scrape down the sides of the bowl occasionally. Add the buttermilk and pulse until just blended, scraping the bowl occasionally.

Pour the batter into the prepared pan and spread it evenly. Scatter the blueberries all over the top and gently push them into the batter. Bake until golden brown and a toothpick inserted into the center of the cake comes out clean, 45 to 50 minutes.

Let cool in the pan on a wire rack. Cut into 8 to 12 squares and serve warm or room temperature.

RHUBARB CAKE

From Kathy Gunst

1¼ pounds fresh rhubarb, cut into ½-inch pieces (about 4 cups)

1½ cups plus ⅓ cup granulated sugar

1 teaspoon pure vanilla extract

½ teaspoon ground ginger

½ teaspoon ground cinnamon

2¼ cups (270 grams) all-purpose flour, plus more for dusting

1 teaspoon baking soda

Pinch of fine salt

1 stick unsalted butter, at room temperature, plus more for buttering

1 large egg

1 cup buttermilk

2 cups strawberries, quartered

Confectioners' sugar, for dusting

In New England, after a long, long winter, rhubarb appears as the first fruit of the season. (Okay, it's officially a vegetable.) The tall pink-red stalks are such a welcome sight, and their distinctive sour flavor is one of my favorites. Most cooks make pie and crisps, but this utterly simple cake was first introduced to me by my friend Rebecca Schultze when our kids were small and time was even shorter. The cake takes about an hour to make from start to finish, making this an ideal cake for any night of the week. I love topping it with macerated strawberries, as seen on page 77.

Position a rack in the center of the oven and preheat the oven to 350°F. Lightly butter a 13 x 9-inch baking pan, then dust it with flour and tap out any excess.

In a medium bowl, combine the rhubarb, ½ cup of the granulated sugar, the vanilla, ginger, and cinnamon and toss to coat. Let sit while you prepare the batter.

In a medium bowl, whisk together the flour, baking soda, and salt.

In a large bowl using an electric mixer, beat the butter and 1 cup of the granulated sugar on medium-high speed until light and fluffy, about 3 minutes. Add the egg and beat well to combine.

With the mixer on low speed, add the flour mixture to the batter in three additions, alternating with the buttermilk, starting and ending with the flour, and beat until just smooth. Gently fold in the rhubarb and the juices with a rubber spatula.

Pour the batter into the prepared pan and spread it out evenly with a spatula. Bake until a toothpick inserted into the center of the cake comes out clean, 50 to 60 minutes.

Meanwhile, toss the strawberries and the ⅓ cup granulated sugar together in a bowl. Set aside while the cake bakes.

Let the cake cool in the pan on a wire rack for 25 to 30 minutes. Cut it into 16 pieces, dust with confectioners' sugar, and serve slightly warm or at room temperature with the strawberries.

SWEDISH VISITING CAKE

From Dorie Greenspan

1 cup sugar, plus more for sprinkling

Finely grated zest of 1 lemon

2 large eggs

¼ teaspoon fine salt

1 teaspoon pure vanilla extract

½ teaspoon pure almond extract

1 cup (120 grams) all-purpose flour

1 stick unsalted butter, melted and cooled

About ¼ cup sliced almonds

We fell in love with this light almond cake (with its golden sugar crust on the outside and soft, chewy moist interior) on first bite. The recipe comes to us from baking goddess Dorie Greenspan, via her friend Ingela Helgesson.

"The first time Ingela came to see us," Dorie tells us, "she arrived with this cake on a flowered platter. 'This is the cake my mother and her friends always brought to one another,' Ingela explained. Then she added that it's also the cake her mother always made when she discovered that company would be coming at a moment's notice. Hence the name Visiting Cake.

"Ingela said that her mother used to claim that you could start making the cake when you saw your guests coming up the road and have it ready by the time they were settling down for coffee. It's only a slight exaggeration."

The cake is an excellent keeper—wrapped well, it can be stored at room temperature for about five days or in the freezer for up to two months.

Position a rack in the center of the oven and preheat the oven to 350°F. Butter a well-seasoned 9-inch cast-iron skillet or another heavy oven-safe skillet, a cake pan, or even a pie pan.

Pour the sugar into a medium bowl. Add the lemon zest and, working with your fingers, blend the zest into the sugar until the sugar is moist and aromatic. Whisk in the eggs one at a time, whisking until each is fully incorporated before adding the next. Whisk in the salt, vanilla, and almond extract. Switch to a rubber spatula and stir in the flour. Finally, fold in the melted butter.

Scrape the batter into the prepared skillet and smooth the top. Scatter the almonds over the top and sprinkle with a little sugar. Bake the cake for 25 to 30 minutes, until it is golden and a little crisp on the outside; the inside will remain moist, even, as Ingela says, "slightly damp." Let the cake cool in the pan for 5 minutes, then run a thin knife around the sides and bottom of the cake to loosen it. You can serve the cake from the skillet or turn it out onto a serving plate and serve warm or at room temperature. Either way, it is meant to be cut into small wedges and eaten sans forks—this is a finger cake.

CAKE WISDOM

ACCURATE MEASURING IS ESSENTIAL for successful cake baking (see Get Out That Scale, page xxi). Too much flour can result in dense cakes.

LINING CAKE PANS: Generally we line cake pans with parchment paper and then butter the parchment or mist it with cooking spray. We use paper liners to make removing cupcakes from tins, cleanup, and transporting the cupcakes easy.

POSITION A RACK IN THE CENTER OF THE OVEN and always preheat the oven for at least 15 minutes before baking.

TEMPERATURE MATTERS: Butter and eggs need to be at the temperature called for in the recipe. At room temperature, they blend with sugar to make an emulsion that suspends air for structure. (One of the smartest things a baking expert shared with us is that air is an ingredient.)

CREAMING BUTTER WITH SUGAR is an important step in creating the structure of a cake. Make sure to stop and scrape the sides of the bowl with a rubber spatula to ensure that the ingredients are evenly combined and nothing is sticking to the bottom of the bowl.

WHEN BEATING WHOLE EGGS OR EGG YOLKS in a cake, beat until the egg falls from the beater in a thick yellow ribbon when the beater is lifted about 5 inches over the surface—the ribbon should hold its shape when it lands on the batter.

ADDING EGGS ONE AT A TIME prevents deflating and ensures even blending and lightness.

IF DIRECTED TO DO SO, ALTERNATING WET AND DRY INGREDIENTS at the end of a recipe is important. This step helps to avoid overmixing, which will result in a leaden cake. Generally, it's best to end with the flour.

FOLDING: Don't overmix. When incorporating ingredients like nuts or chocolate chips into a cake batter, it's best to fold them in versus stirring them to combine. To fold, draw the broad side of a rubber spatula through the center of the batter like an oar through water. Turn the bowl a quarter turn with each stroke to evenly pull the ingredients from the bottom.

DON'T DILLYDALLY: As soon as a batter is combined, transfer it to the pan and get it into the oven to avoid the batter deflating.

WHEN BAKING MULTIPLE CAKE LAYERS, rotate the pans halfway through the baking time, but don't leave the oven door open long enough to let the temperature drop.

CAKE TESTERS, TOOTHPICKS, OR THIN WOODEN SKEWERS are helpful to inspect the moisture and finished crumb on a cake. Every oven is a little different, so it's important to go by the visual cues as well as the timing indicated in the recipe.

COOL ON A RACK: It's very important to let cakes cool completely. Run a knife around the edge of a cake before turning it out of a pan. Turn the pan over onto a flat plate or cake stand. If the cake is sticking, it's often better to tap the bottom of the pan to let gravity take over than to force the cake out of the pan and potentially break it. That said, if your cake doesn't come out in one piece, don't fret. Put the offending piece back in place and cover it with frosting, glaze, or confectioners' sugar.

MANY CAKES ARE ACTUALLY BETTER THE NEXT DAY as they "ripen" and the crumb sets.

BRUSH THE CAKE WITH A PASTRY BRUSH to remove loose crumbs before frosting. Don't try to frost a warm cake; the frosting will soften and droop and you will be sad. When glazing a cake, set a wire rack over a sheet of parchment paper or waxed paper, a plate, pan, or bowl, then set the cake on the rack and glaze; the paper or vessel underneath will catch the runoff, making cleanup easier.

ROTATING CAKE STANDS: These stands are nice to have if you bake a lot of cakes or are into cake decorating, and they also make for a dramatic presentation. Lay some strips of parchment paper on the stand under the edge of the cake; remove them when you've finished frosting the cake. This will keep the cake stand clean and will create a clean edge around the bottom of the finished cake.

WHEN FROSTING CAKES OR ASSEMBLING A LAYER CAKE, invert the cake or cake layers so the smooth flat side (the side that was at the bottom of the pan) is up. If the cake or cake layer is very domed, you can trim the top with a serrated knife. If using a soft filling like whipped cream between cake layers, don't spread it all the way to the edge; the filling will spread when the next layer is placed on top. When frosting a cake, do what the pros do and crumb coat your cake: Start by applying a very thin layer of frosting all over the cake, then refrigerate for 10 to 15 minutes before applying the remaining frosting. This seals the cake and prevents crumbs from getting into the outer layer of frosting.

AN OFFSET METAL SPATULA is a great tool for frosting cakes. Start from the top and spread frosting to the edges; overflow can then be spread on the sides. It's best to add a generous dollop to the center of the cake and push the frosting over to the edges. It's not essential to frost the sides of a cake. For a smooth side, hold the offset spatula perpendicular to the cake and turn the cake to make a clean edge. A bench scraper is a great tool for making smooth edges as well. To make swirls in frosting, use the back of a spoon.

THE SIDES OF A CAKE can be finished with chopped nuts, sprinkles, coconut, chocolate curls, toasted cake crumbs, or whole or crumbled cookies. Generally the decorations should be an indication of the flavor of cake. For example, in Kathy's Chocolate Raspberry Triple-Layer Cake (page 101), fresh raspberries would be appropriate, while something like chocolate-covered coffee beans might muddle the flavors.

A PASTRY BAG is not essential for cake decorating (see page 99), but having a medium pastry bag with a couple of tips can make finishing a cupcake or cake fast work, not to mention make it look impressive. To fill a pastry bag, drop the tip into the bag (or, if you are into multiple tips, attach it to a "coupler," which allows you to easily switch between tips). Set the pastry bag in a tall glass or quart container and fold back the top of the bag by 3 to 5 inches. Scoop the frosting into the bag with a rubber spatula. Unfold the top and twist the bag shut, pushing the frosting into the tip and down toward the front of the bag. Hold the bag at a 45-degree angle about an inch or so from the surface being decorated. Apply pressure from the back of the bag and let the frosting fall easily, like a rope; avoid dragging or pulling the frosting.

IF YOU WANT TO ADD COLOR TO WHITE FROSTING, tint it with food coloring. We prefer gel colors for their intensity. Remember, a little bit of food coloring goes a long way. You can find tubes of gel color and colored edible frosting at many craft stores and online (see Mail-Order Rage on page 163).

CAKE CARRIERS ARE GREAT FOR TRANSPORTING CAKES. If you don't have one, inverting a large bowl (large enough that it does not touch the top of the cake) over the cake plate can be a good stand-in. Tape the edges in place if traveling with the cake. This is also a good way to store a cake without disturbing the frosting. Another way is to insert a couple of toothpicks into the top of the cake and drape plastic or reusable wrap over the cake; the toothpicks keep the wrap from touching the surface.

CAKES WITH GLAZES CAN BE STORED AT ROOM TEMPERATURE. Cakes with whipped cream or other dairy-based frostings or fillings should be stored in the refrigerator. Always bring a cake to room temperature before serving; this takes 15 minutes to 1 hour, depending on the heat of the day.

CUPCAKES CAN BE FINISHED by placing a scoop of frosting on top (see below).

Cupcake Tip!

This may sound like woo-woo voodoo, but it works: A very easy way to decorate a cupcake is to use a small ice cream or cookie scoop to place a ball of frosting on top. Very lightly tap the cake or cupcake on the counter and, like magic, the frosting will settle evenly over the top.

SPICED PARSNIP CUPCAKES
with **MAPLE CREAM FROSTING**

From Kathy Gunst

For the Cupcakes

Cooking spray (optional)

1 cup walnut pieces

1½ cups (180 grams) all-purpose flour

¾ cup granulated sugar

2 tablespoons finely chopped crystallized ginger

2 teaspoons baking powder

1 teaspoon ground cinnamon

½ teaspoon ground ginger

½ teaspoon freshly grated nutmeg

½ teaspoon fine salt

¼ teaspoon ground allspice

3 large eggs

½ cup vegetable oil

½ cup buttermilk

4 or 5 parsnips (11 ounces), peeled and shredded on the largest holes of a grater

For the Frosting

8 ounces cream cheese, at room temperature

¾ stick (6 tablespoons) unsalted butter, at room temperature

¾ teaspoon pure vanilla extract

⅓ cup confectioners' sugar

2 tablespoons pure maple syrup

2 tablespoons crystallized ginger, cut into thin slivers

I adore carrot cake, but wondered what it might be like to shake things up a bit. Parsnips, like carrots, are a root vegetable with all kinds of earthy nuance and natural sweetness. Here they are made into a cupcake topped with maple syrup frosting, toasted nuts, and crystallized ginger.

Position a rack in the center of the oven and preheat the oven to 350°F. Spray a 12-cup muffin tin with cooking spray, making sure to butter the bottom and sides, or drop in paper liners.

Toast the walnuts on a baking sheet, about 8 minutes. Cool. Finely chop half the walnuts and set aside; coarsely chop the remaining walnuts.

Make the cupcakes: Whisk the flour, granulated sugar, crystallized ginger, and baking powder in a large bowl. Add the cinnamon, ground ginger, nutmeg, salt, and allspice and combine.

Whisk the eggs in a medium bowl. Add the oil and buttermilk and whisk to combine evenly. Add the egg mixture to the flour mixture along with the parsnips and the *coarsely chopped* walnuts. Divide the batter among the muffin cups, filling each about two-thirds full. Bake until a toothpick inserted in the center o a cupcake comes out clean, 20 to 25 minutes. Cool on a rack for 5 to 10 minutes, then remove from the tin.

Make the frosting: Working with an electric mixer beat the cream cheese and butter in a large bowl, until fully blended and light, about 1 minute. Add the vanilla, confectioners' sugar, and maple syrup and mix until smooth. Refrigerate for about 30 minutes to firm it up.

Generously frost the top of the cupcakes and sprinkle with the finely chopped walnuts and add a sliver of the candied ginger.

(DON'T CALL ME)
HONEY CAKES

From Katherine Alford

For the Cupcakes

Cooking spray or oil, for buttering (optional)

2 cups (240 grams) all-purpose flour

1½ teaspoons baking powder

½ teaspoon freshly grated nutmeg

¼ teaspoon fine salt

⅛ teaspoon baking soda

¾ cup sugar

6 tablespoons unsalted butter, cut in small pieces, at room temperature

⅔ cup plain whole-milk yogurt (not Greek)

⅔ cup honey

2 large eggs, at room temperature

2 tablespoons vegetable oil

1 teaspoon pure vanilla extract

For the Frosting

12 ounces cream cheese, at room temperature

¾ cup confectioners' sugar

⅓ cup honey

1 teaspoon pure vanilla extract

1 teaspoon fresh lemon juice

Honeycomb Candy (recipe follows; optional), for garnish

We have all been there. Some dude thinks it's okay to call you "honey," "sweetie," or "babe." You might blanch or glare or just ignore him, but it sets a tone. Many men have bemoaned to me recently that they aren't sure how to talk to women anymore. Seriously? It's time they all just listen.

These cakes feature the flavor of honey without being overly cloying or sweet. The homemade honeycomb candy, although not essential, is a cool addition. If you have never seen how baking soda reacts in hot sugar, this is kitchen science in action. If there ever was a visual metaphor for how you feel about all those dudes calling you "sweetie," it is this volcanic, seething, bubbling hot sugar.

Position a rack in the center of the oven and preheat the oven to 350°F. Line a 12-cup muffin tin with paper liners, mist each cup with cooking spray, or butter with oil.

Make the cupcakes: In the bowl of a stand mixer, whisk together the flour, baking powder, nutmeg, salt, and baking soda. Add the sugar, attach the paddle attachment, and mix well. Add the butter and mix until the mixture looks slightly yellow and the butter is evenly incorporated.

In a large liquid measuring cup, whisk the yogurt, honey, eggs, oil, and vanilla until thoroughly combined. Add the yogurt mixture to the flour mixture and mix until blended, 20 to 30 seconds.

Scoop about ⅓ cup of the batter into each prepared muffin cup. Bake until golden brown and a toothpick inserted into the center of a cupcake comes out clean, about 20 minutes. Let cool in the tin on a wire rack for 5 minutes. Unmold and transfer the cupcakes to the rack and let cool completely.

Meanwhile, make the frosting: In a stand mixer fitted with the paddle attachment, combine all the frosting ingredients and beat on medium speed until light and smooth, about 2 minutes. Cover and refrigerate until firm, about 1 hour.

Pipe, spoon, or generously spread the frosting on the cooled cupcakes. Top each with a piece of honeycomb candy just before serving.

HONEYCOMB CANDY

½ cup sugar

¼ cup light corn syrup

2 tablespoons honey

2 tablespoons water

1 teaspoon baking soda

Line an 8-inch square baking pan with parchment paper, leaving a couple of inches of parchment overhanging the sides.

In a heavy-bottomed small saucepan, combine the sugar, corn syrup, honey, and water. (Make sure the saucepan doesn't have shallow sides because the sugar will foam up a lot.) Whisk together and then set over medium-high heat. Attach a candy thermometer to the side of the pan and cook, without stirring (it's okay to swirl the pan if the sugar starts to brown unevenly) until the sugar reaches 290° to 300°F. Remove from the heat and immediately whisk in the baking soda—it will foam up epically. Quickly pour the mixture into the prepared baking pan and set aside to cool completely, about 30 minutes. Break or cut the candy into pieces. Store in an airtight container at room temperature for a day or two. Heads up: If it's humid, the candy will get tacky and soft.

BURNT
RED VELVET CUPCAKES

From Katherine Alford

For the Cupcakes

Cooking spray (optional)

1¼ cups (150 grams) cake flour

3 tablespoons unsweetened
Dutch-process cocoa powder

1 teaspoon baking powder

¼ teaspoon fine salt

2 tablespoons safflower
or vegetable oil

2 tablespoons unsalted butter,
at room temperature

¾ cup granulated sugar

1 large egg

½ teaspoon pure vanilla extract

½ cup buttermilk

1 teaspoon red gel food coloring

¼ teaspoon baking soda

¼ teaspoon apple cider vinegar

For the Frosting

8 large marshmallows

8 ounces cream cheese,
at room temperature

2 tablespoons unsalted butter

¼ teaspoon pure vanilla extract

⅓ to ½ cup confectioners' sugar

Red velvet cake, with its vibrant red cocoa layers and creamy frosting, made a comeback in the new millennium. They are a playful, super-girly, retro classic. But they took on new meaning when the red robes and white wimple of Margaret Atwood's feminist allegory, The Handmaid's Tale, captured the insidious erosion of women's freedoms. These are great for your next book club meeting when you're rereading this powerful and disturbing work of fiction, which these days feels all too real. We add a little char to the frosting with toasted marshmallows for a slightly subversive take.

Gel food coloring used to be available only in specialty food shops, but now you may be able to find it in your grocery or craft store, and if not, check out Mail-Order Rage (page 163); they are more vibrant than the weak liquid food coloring we all grew up with.

Position a rack in the center of the oven and preheat the oven to 350°F. Line a 12-cup muffin tin with paper liners or lightly spray with cooking spray.

Make the cupcakes: Whisk together the flour, cocoa powder, baking powder, and salt, in a medium bowl.

In a stand mixer fitted with the paddle attachment, beat the oil and butter on medium speed until combined (it's okay if the butter and oil don't emulsify completely). Add the granulated sugar and beat on medium-high until light and fluffy, about 2 minutes more. Add the egg and vanilla and beat until fully incorporated.

In a liquid measuring cup, mix the buttermilk and red food coloring.

With the mixer on low speed, add the flour mixture in three additions, alternating with the buttermilk, beginning and ending with the flour. Mix until well combined.

continued

In a small bowl, mix the baking soda and vinegar until it foams, then very lightly fold it into the batter by hand. Scoop the batter into the prepared tin, filling each cup about halfway. Bake until a toothpick inserted into the center of a cupcake comes out clean, about 20 minutes. Let cool in the tin on a wire rack for about 5 minutes, then transfer the un-molded cupcakes to the rack to cool.

Make the frosting: Switch the oven to broil. Line a small oven-safe pan or skillet with aluminum foil. Arrange the marshmallows in the pan. Broil, turning as needed using small tongs, until golden brown, 1 to 2 minutes (depending on how charred you like your marshmallows). Let cool.

In a stand mixer fitted with the paddle attachment, beat the cream cheese and butter on medium speed until light and smooth, about 1 minute. Add the vanilla and confectioners' sugar and beat until well blended. Add the charred marshmallows and beat until barely incorporated.

Use a 2-tablespoon cookie or ice cream scoop to place a mound of frosting on top of each cupcake. Tap the cupcakes on the counter so the frosting settles evenly over the top. (Alternatively, transfer the frosting to a piping bag and pipe it onto the cupcakes.)

ALMOND AND CHOCOLATE LECHE CAKE
(PASTEL DE ALMENDRAS Y CHOCOLATE DE LECHE)

From Pati Jinich

6 ounces bittersweet chocolate

2 sticks unsalted butter,
plus more for buttering

4 large eggs

2 cups sweetened condensed milk

1½ cups (180 grams) almond flour

½ teaspoon baking soda

½ teaspoon baking powder

Pinch of kosher or coarse sea salt

¼ cup boiling water

Confectioners' sugar, for dusting

Pati is an award-winning chef and the host of the TV show Pati's Mexican Table. This is the kind of cake that looks and tastes like it took you all day to make. But it's so simple to put together and is light and not too sweet. It also has the benefit of being gluten-free, and is made with almond flour, chocolate, butter, and sweetened condensed milk.

Position a rack in the center of the oven and preheat the oven to 350°F. Butter the bottom and sides of a 9-inch springform pan, line the bottom with parchment paper cut to fit, and butter the parchment.

Put the chocolate and butter in a heatproof medium bowl and set it over a small saucepan of barely simmering water (make sure the bottom of the bowl doesn't touch the water). Stir occasionally until melted and combined, about 2 minutes. (Alternatively, combine the chocolate and butter in a microwave-safe bowl and microwave in 20-second bursts, stirring after each, until melted and combined.)

Put the eggs and condensed milk in a blender and blend until smooth. Add the melted chocolate and blend to combine. Transfer the mixture to a large bowl. Whisk in the almond flour, baking soda, baking powder, and salt and mix well. Add the boiling water and whisk until smooth.

Pour the batter into the prepared pan and bake until the top is fluffy and springy to the touch, and a toothpick inserted into the center of the cake comes out moist but not wet, 40 to 45 minutes. Let cool in the pan on a wire rack for 10 minutes. Remove the springform ring and let the cake cool to room temperature on the rack.

Carefully flip the cake onto a plate, remove the bottom of the pan and the parchment, then flip again so the cake is right-side up. Dust the top with confectioners' sugar and serve.

FEMINISM, FAMILY,
AND THE F-WORD

A CONVERSATION WITH KATIE ANTHONY

Katie Anthony writes about feminism, family, and other F-words in her blog KatyKatiKate *and other publications.*

KATHY GUNST: How does the word "rage" resonate with you?

KATIE ANTHONY: Rage is a tool, one that I, like many women, learned to use later in life. Before I could get comfortable with my hand around the handle of rage, I had to learn how to laugh at the idea that only "crazy bitches" get mad. I love my rage. It's better than coffee to keep me grinding. It's better than knowledge to keep me focused on what matters. It's better than fear to get my ass in gear.

KATHY: How do you use rage to manuever through the world?

KATIE: Rage works. It's an incredible tool, but like any tool, you have to know when to pick it up and when to put it down. While rage helps me grind, it also grinds the wrong thing if I let it roll unchecked. Hot takes are rarely nuanced, and everything that matters is complicated. While rage gets my ass in gear, it will burn me to ash if I don't cool off from time to time.

KATHY: How important is humor in your writing?

KATIE: The worse it gets out there, the more we need humor. Think about it: What are jokes? Jokes can be distractions or tension breakers. They can be energizers, connectors, translators, or weapons. They can be mirrors, reflecting hard truths back

to us with a spoonful of sugar to help the medicine go down. They can be windows, giving us a glimpse of other people's experiences. Good jokes make people feel good while they also do the hard work of energizing people in pain, connecting us to each other so we don't feel alone, translating experiences to break silence, and creating empathy for people we don't yet understand.

We are living in a time when the personhood of women is under constant negotiation, black people continue to die in acts of unaccountable state violence (Tamir Rice would have turned seventeen this year), and child immigrants at our border meet abject cruelty at the hands of American government employees. Humor is the freaking duct tape of society in times of fear and uncertainty, and hi, hello, we're there.

KATHY: It seems you have to be so careful with the stories you tell, even in jokes. I mean, who owns our stories?

KATIE: Appropriating other people's experiences to tell jokes about a life I don't live isn't cool. For example, I wouldn't write a joke about the trans experience, even if I were punching up at a transphobic lawmaker trying to push through a bathroom bill. If I wrote a joke about the trans experience and it got laughs, I would become a cisgender writer who capitalized on a lived trans experience to delight my largely cisgender readership, despite the fact that neither I nor most of my readers will ever experience the very real danger of navigating public spaces as a trans person. I would have plucked the joke out of the life, as inappropriately as if I'd plucked the cherry out of someone else's Manhattan. That's not my joke to tell. Line crossed.

KATHY: Can you talk about the collection of essays in your book, *Feminist Werewolf*? What is a feminist werewolf?

KATIE: After my first viral blog post, a rant about Harvey Weinstein that hit in 2017, readers sent me money. I got offers to write for big outlets. I was invited to speak on sexual violence on our local NPR station. My professional life benefited from a piece I'd written excoriating a man who'd abused countless women.

A rant has value and I don't feel guilty about writing it, but I did get very uncomfortable with the disproportionate amount of attention going to me, a writer who had never met Weinstein and had no reason to fear retaliation from the Hollywood power structure after I called Weinstein a "scaly rhino dong." I felt that the women who were survivors deserved more support than I did because they were the ones who'd really risked something by speaking out. I pulled together a number of pieces I'd written about rape culture, feminism, street harassment, you name it, and I self-published it on Amazon as the collection *Feminist Werewolf*. One hundred percent of the proceeds from *Feminist Werewolf* go to anti-sexual violence organizations.

The title is rooted in the idea that many people have a feminist werewolf who lives inside them. Mine is mean and merciless and fresh out of fucks. I didn't choose her; she was given to me against my will out of trauma and shame and fear. I had to learn how to live with her inside me, and I even came to be grateful that she existed even if I know I will never be grateful for the traumas that gave her to me.

KATHY: How do you keep your anger from getting the best of you?

KATIE: If you don't keep an eye on your anger, you'll start to feel satisfied by the intensity of your fury and mistake your satisfaction for evidence that you've actually done something impactful. One of the greatest lessons I learned early in my anti-racism education is that white people don't get points for being willing to talk about racism. You'll often hear well-meaning people say things like, "But isn't it great that we're having these con-versations? Isn't that progress?" Sure, conversations are great, but they're not actions.

KATHY: You're the mother of two. Do you ever get time to bake? What's life like in your kitchen?

KATIE: I believe that baking, writing, and parenting are the same thing, and I do them all in my kitchen/office/command center. I'm raising two sons; I'm baking lasagna; I'm writing an essay. I'm reminding my sons to say please; I'm dicing another onion; I'm typing the words, "Calm down, Katie. What are you really trying to say?" I'm reading the parenting book, the chapter about biting; I'm checking the recipe; I'm reading someone else's better writing.

At the end of the labor I hope to be able to give you a bubbling pan of lasagna that will hold together when it's served, a kind child who will not grow up to be a flaming asshole, a decent read that will help you laugh or learn or feel powerful. But you know, sometimes the miracle doesn't arrive. Sometimes dinner is a box of mac and cheese, the kids are alive and no further promises can be made, and the best thing we can say about the essay is that it is indeed composed of words.

> *"I love my rage. It's better than coffee to keep me grinding."*

KATHY: What gives you hope these days?

KATIE: Lots of things give me hope: Large donations, crowdfunded summer meals for children who rely on school for food, Academy Award winners who aren't just white men, interspecies animal friendships, the normalization of a woman's round body on television. For me, the question is not "Where can I find hope?" but rather "What will I do once I've found it again?"

Hope is out there. We're not short on hope. But we're also not short on pain, which is why I think we have to start thinking of hope not as a respite, but as a refill. We have to start thinking of pain not as something to avoid, but as a necessary part of our humanity, the place that burns to let us know we need help.

ALMOND CAKE
with RICOTTA AND JAM
(TORTA DI MANDORLA CON CREMA
DI RICOTTA E MARMELLATA)

From Domenica Marchetti

For the Cake

1 stick unsalted butter, melted and cooled

4 large eggs

1 cup granulated sugar

½ teaspoon pure vanilla extract

½ teaspoon pure almond extract

1 cup (100 grams) almond flour

1 cup (120 grams) cake flour

¼ teaspoon fine salt

For the Ricotta Cream Filling

⅔ cup cold ricotta cheese

⅔ cup cold heavy cream

½ cup cold mascarpone cheese

¼ cup confectioners' sugar

¼ teaspoon pure vanilla extract

To Assemble

½ to ¾ cup strawberry or raspberry jam at room temperature

"It's difficult to single out one instance of outrage since 2016," writes cookbook author Domenica Marchetti. "But the one that stands out for me is the Unite the Right rally that took place in Charlottesville in August 2017. I was on a road trip, and I sat in disbelief in the passenger seat chasing Twitter links on my phone about the tiki-torch-carrying white nationalists who marched across the campus of UVA on Friday night. On Saturday they took their polo-shirt, khaki-clad hate parade to the streets of Charlottesville. Three people—a thirty-two-year-old woman and two state troopers—died as a result of the neo-Nazis' assault on the city.

"I have lived in Virginia for nearly twenty-five years. So this story hit me hard. But two and a half months after that dreadful event, Virginia had a blue wave election. Among those swept into the state's general assembly were fifteen women, including Virginia's first openly transgender woman, first openly lesbian delegate, first Asian American delegate, and first two Latina delegates.

"Can a cake be gentle? This one seems to be; it has a gentle almond flavor and a tender crumb. Once baked and cooled, it is sliced in half and spread with a layer of jam and a cloud of whipped ricotta cream. There is no added leavening in this cake; it relies on the air beaten into the eggs. So you'll need a light hand and a certain amount of care not to deflate the batter as you fold in the dry ingredients; and beyond that, a little bit of faith that once you set it in the oven, it will rise."

Position a rack in the center of the oven and preheat the oven to 325°F. Brush an 8-inch springform pan with melted butter, then line the bottom with parchment paper and butter as well.

Make the cake: Whisk the eggs and granulated sugar in the bowl of a stand mixer fitted with the whisk attachment on low speed to combine, then whisk on high until the mixture is pale yellow, thick, and airy, about 2 minutes. Beat in the vanilla and almond extract.

continued

In a medium bowl, sift together the almond flour, cake flour, and salt to remove any clumps. With a large rubber spatula, gently fold the flour mixture into the whipped egg mixture, taking care to use light strokes. Fold in the melted butter using the same light movements. Scrape the batter into the prepared pan. Bake for 50 to 55 minutes, until a cake tester inserted into the center comes out clean. Let the cake cool in the pan on a wire rack for 10 minutes. Run a knife around the edge of the cake, then remove the springform ring. Let the cake cool for 20 minutes more, then carefully invert it onto a plate and remove the bottom of the pan and the parchment. Flip the cake again so it's right-side up and let cool to room temperature.

Meanwhile, make the ricotta cream. Spoon the ricotta into a fine-mesh sieve set over the bowl of a stand mixer and use a spoon to press the ricotta through the sieve. Add the cream, mascarpone, confectioners' sugar, and vanilla and beat on high for 60 to 90 seconds, until the mixture holds stiff peaks.

Assemble the cake: Set the cooled cake on a clean work surface and, using a serrated knife, carefully slice it in half horizontally to make two layers. Transfer the bottom half of the cake, cut-side up, to a serving plate or cake stand. Spread the jam over the cake, covering the entire surface. Spread a thick layer of the ricotta cream on top of the jam, again covering the entire surface to the edge.

Gently set the top half of the cake, cut-side down, over the ricotta cream. Cover the entire cake with the remaining ricotta cream. Cover with plastic or reusable wrap and refrigerate for several hours or up to overnight to allow the cake to soak up a bit of moisture from the jam and cream filling.

To serve, remove the cake from the refrigerator and let sit at room temperature for about 1 hour. Use a serrated knife to slice it into wedges, without pressing down too heavily on the cake.

MY TWO MOTHERS

I had two mothers. Not the loving lesbian kind, but two women, one black, one white, who came together by circumstance. When I was a toddler, my father took a powder (aka vanished, disappeared; let's just say there were private detectives involved). My mother, Carolyn, was left a single parent with three young daughters in a New Jersey suburb. In the few faded pictures from those years, we look like missing characters from a *Mad Men* episode. And like women in Don and Betty's world, my mother suffered the harsh stigma of being the "divorcée." Although she was from a respected, well-off family, active in local politics—she was the youngest delegate at the 1956 Republican convention—she had fallen from privilege. Neighbors' husbands pushed her to "get a little something on the side." With no job or college degree (she dropped out to marry my father), she packed us all up and moved us to Washington, DC. It was 1960, Kennedy had just been elected, and like so many she felt the world was possible.

That first week in DC, Virginia came into our lives. Years later she told me that when she first saw us, she thought, *Whoa, these girls need me*. She was right. She brought stability, kindness, humor, discipline, and amazing food. She would say she was "country" and had her own story of why she left a family behind. My mother found a job, and Virginia took care of my sisters and me; together, they made our home a safe place. This was no small feat in DC in the 1960s.

I was six when Kennedy was assassinated. My mother, sisters, and I stood on a curb with weeping women mourners with beehive hairdos and watched his funeral cortege pass. I remember asking, "Why are the empty boots backward in the horse's stirrups?" My mother tried to explain how this was a way to honor a fallen soldier, but she choked up before I understood. This was the start of an accelerating confusion in the country that became my norm. Johnson, Vietnam, Nixon, Martin, Bobby, Kent State, Jackson State . . . I grew to expect protests, marches, martial law, nightly curfews, learned to avoid tear gas and cross National Guard barricades to get to school. The need and right to dissent, to speak up, was all around me. When the FBI came to our door to investigate our neighbors, my mother threw them out.

Afternoons spent in the kitchen with Virginia became a refuge of laughter, connection, and hours literally exploring the joys of cooking. She taught me the importance of measuring, how to work a hand grinder to make croquettes, how to frost a cake. I loved it and her. One day when I was around nine, I came home to find the kitchen covered with baked goods. There was a German chocolate cake, swirled Bundts, triple-layered coconut bars, Boston cream pie, brownies, cookies, and more. It was as if the dessert chapters from the *Joy of Cooking* had jumped off their pages and into our kitchen. "I bake when I am mad," Virginia said with a strange calm. This had clearly been an epic rage. Her anger—blended with flour, butter, and sugar—expressed more than that saccharine cliché of "baking with love." It had power. I learned to respect rage. Not to mention skilled baking. As a child I couldn't fully grasp the roots of her anger, but as a black woman in America the list was, and continues to be, endlessly long.

My mother was not a baker. The one time she made a cake, it had an inedible frosting made with unsweetened chocolate. But food could be a tool for her as well. When Martin Luther King Jr. was assassinated, we grieved, and watched as Washington erupted in a righteous rage. The 14th Street corridor became a war zone—fires, looting, police dogs, and National Guard occupation. The city came to an anxious halt. My mother, never passive, started cooking. She organized a food drive for the African American community affected by the riots. She called friends, her church, our neighbors, but many of these "fine" people hung up on her. Undeterred, we pulled out every edible thing in the house and started making sandwiches, casseroles, whatever we could concoct. (Canned salmon will forever remind me of 1968.) After three days of nonstop cooking, my sisters and I were enlisted to pack up our lemon yellow station wagon. My mother drove to the inner city, alone, and somehow talked her way through the police barricades to share food with a physically and emotionally devastated community. At ten, I felt useful in a world that was spinning with rage.

Growing up in a home of all women was something I took for granted. I don't anymore. It allowed me to have a voice, not to tamp it down, and be heard. At one point we all were in school—elementary for me, middle and high school for my sisters, my mother back in college, and Virginia studying for a GED. I felt like we were all in it together. Virginia worked for us for over a decade. She married—my sister and I were honored bridesmaids in her wedding—had a son, and then moved on in her life to a better job. We are still in touch today and she calls us "my girls." I owe her a grounded sense of what it means to move through the world with integrity.

My mother and I didn't agree on politics, but she did teach me to show up with what you have, stand up for what you believe in, be brave, and "screw the bigots." Decades later, I sat by her hospital bed. She had suffered a stroke and struggled to speak. The room was still, except for the TV pundits discussing Supreme Court nominee Samuel Alito and his position on *Roe v. Wade*. Suddenly my mother spoke clearly and distinctly. "It's no one's fucking business what a woman does with her body!" I laughed and then I cried, "Right on, Carolyn!" Her moxie inspires me today.

When I think about Rage Baking, both of my mothers are equal parts of the recipe.

NOT TAKING ANY MORE
"SHEET" CAKE

From Katherine Alford

For the Cake

Cooking spray (optional)

2½ cups (300 grams) cake flour
or all-purpose flour, plus more for dusting

1¾ cups granulated sugar

1 tablespoon baking powder

½ teaspoon fine salt

2½ sticks unsalted butter, cut into
cubes and chilled

⅔ cup whole milk

4 large eggs, beaten

1 tablespoon pure vanilla extract

For the Vanilla Frosting

2 sticks unsalted butter, at room
temperature, but on the firm side

4 cups confectioners sugar, sifted

¼ cup light cream

2 to 3 teaspoons pure vanilla extract

Juice of ½ lemon

Gel food coloring (optional)

For the Fruit Frosting

1 ounce freeze-dried fruit,
such as raspberries

1½ cups heavy cream

⅓ cup confectioners' sugar

Decorating gel, for writing

This is an easy, go-to cake that can be put together in no time. Sheet cakes are a great open canvas for whatever message you want to share. Get creative and expressive. Bring your rage or celebration; the message can be soft, rageful, funny, decorative, playful, or proud. Right now, VOTE! and #NeverthelessShePersisted comes to mind. Pipe the edges, add sprinkles, candy, fruit, edible flowers, or flags. Go for it! We give two options for the frosting— make one or both if you want to step up the decorating.

Position a rack in the center of the oven and preheat the oven to 350°F. Line a 13 x 9-inch baking pan with parchment paper, leaving a couple of inches of parchment overhanging the sides. Lightly butter the parchment and dust it with flour, tapping out any excess, or mist it with cooking spray.

Make the cake: In a large food processor, combine the flour, granulated sugar, baking powder, and salt and pulse 4 or 5 times to combine. Add the butter and pulse 5 to 7 times, until the flour turns sandy with some pieces of butter still visible. (Alternatively, in a stand mixer fitted with the paddle attachment, mix the flour, sugar, baking powder, and salt on low speed until combined. Add the butter and mix on medium speed until powdery.)

In a medium bowl or liquid measuring cup, whisk together the milk, eggs, and vanilla. With the food processor running (or with the stand mixer on medium speed), pour the milk mixture into the flour mixture and process until smooth.

Pour the batter into the prepared pan, smooth the top with an offset spatula. Bake until a toothpick inserted into the center of the cake comes out clean, 25 to 30 minutes. Let the cake cool in the pan on a wire rack for 5 minutes. Use the overhanging parchment to lift the cake from the pan and set it on the rack to cool completely.

continued

Meanwhile, make the vanilla frosting: In a stand mixer fitted with the paddle attachment, beat the butter on medium-high speed until light and fluffy. With the mixer on low speed, add the confectioners' sugar and light cream, then add the vanilla and lemon juice and beat until light and fluffy. Tint part or all of the frosting with a few drops of food coloring, if desired.

And/or make the fruit frosting: Pulse the freeze-dried fruit to a powder in the food processor. Add the heavy cream and confectioners' sugar and process until combined and thickened, about 1 minute.

Trim the edges of the cake, if uneven. Use an offset spatula to spread the frosting over the top. Decorate as desired. Use gel frosting to write a Rage Baking message that speaks to you!

I Don't Need A Fancy Pastry Bag, Do I?

You've seen the chef with the tall toque on top of his head, holding a fancy pastry bag and squiggling out all kinds of fancy and intimidating shapes and patterns. And you've thought: **Nope, not me. I'm not getting into that fancy-ass pastry bag thing!**

But wait . . . you know that little resealable sandwich bag you have in your kitchen drawer? Yes, that one. Fill the bag with your icing or batter, cut the tiniest hole in one corner, squeeze out all the air, and begin piping. What, you say? Seriously, is it really that simple? Yes, sometimes it really is. You can thank us later.

CHOCOLATE RASPBERRY
TRIPLE-LAYER CAKE

From Kathy Gunst

For the Cake

1 cup unsweetened Dutch-process cocoa powder

2 cups boiling water

2⅔ cups (320 grams) sifted all-purpose flour, plus more for dusting

2 teaspoons baking soda

½ teaspoon baking powder

½ teaspoon fine salt

2 sticks unsalted butter, at room temperature, plus more for buttering

2½ cups granulated sugar

4 large eggs, at room temperature

1½ teaspoons pure vanilla extract

For the Frosting

½ cup heavy cream

2 sticks unsalted butter, cut into pieces

6 ounces bittersweet or semisweet chocolate or a combination, finely chopped

½ cup confectioners' sugar, sifted if clumpy

One of my oldest friends Elisa Newman made me this cake a few years ago, and I thought it was perfect. She got the recipe from her friend Marguerite Horwath, who found it in a 1950s McCalls Cooking School publication. (Don't all cakes have long lineage?) Trust me when I say this cake is well worth your time. The cake and the frosting can be made a day ahead.

Position two racks evenly in the oven and preheat the oven to 350°F. Line the bottoms of three 9-inch round cake pans with parchment paper cut to fit. Brush the parchment and the sides of the pans liberally with butter, then dust them lightly with flour and tap out any excess.

Make the cake: Sift the cocoa powder into a medium bowl. While whisking, pour in the boiling water and whisk until smooth. Let cool completely.

Sift the flour, baking soda, baking powder, and salt into another medium bowl.

In a stand mixer fitted with the paddle attachment, beat the butter and granulated sugar on medium speed until light and fluffy, about 3 minutes. Add the eggs one at a time, beating until each is fully incorporated before adding the next, then add the vanilla. Increase the mixer speed to medium-high and beat until light and very fluffy, about 5 minutes.

With the mixer on low speed, add the flour mixture in four additions, alternating with the cocoa mixture, beginning and ending with the flour. Take care not to overbeat the batter. Divide the batter evenly among the prepared pans.

Bake the cakes, rotating the pans halfway through baking, until a toothpick inserted into the center comes out clean, about 25 minutes. Let cool in the pans on a wire rack for 10 minutes. Carefully invert the cakes onto a plate, then flip again so the cakes are right-side up. Return the cakes to the rack, parchment-side down, and let cool completely.

Make the frosting: In a small saucepan, stir together the cream and butter over medium heat until the butter melts and the mixture simmers. Off the heat, whisk in chocolate and confectioners' sugar until melted and smooth. Transfer

continued

CHOCOLATE RASPBERRY TRIPLE-LAYER CAKE

(continued)

For the Filling

1 cup cold heavy cream

¼ to ⅓ cup confectioners' sugar, sifted

1 teaspoon pure vanilla extract

½ cup seedless raspberry jam

To Assemble

Fresh raspberries, chocolate pearls, sprinkles, candied or edible flowers, or candy

to a bowl and cool to room temperature, stirring periodically. Cover and refrigerate until thick, about 1 hour. (The cake and frosting can be covered and refrigerated overnight and assembled the next day.)

Make the filling: In a stand mixer fitted with the whisk attachment, beat the cream on medium speed until it holds soft peaks. Add the confectioners' sugar and vanilla and beat until the cream holds a slightly stiff peak. Cover and refrigerate while you whip the frosting.

Assemble the cake: Beat the chilled frosting in a stand mixer fitted with the whisk attachment on medium speed until light and fluffy, 2 to 3 minutes.

Place one cake layer top-side down on a large round serving plate or cake stand. Remove the parchment. Gently spread half the jam in the center of the cake, leaving about a ¾-inch border. Add half the whipped cream, again leaving about a ¾-inch border. Place a second cake layer top-side down, remove the parchment, and repeat with the remaining jam and cream. Place the third layer, top-side down, and remove the parchment.

Spread a very thin layer of the frosting evenly over the sides and top of the cake with an offset spatula. Refrigerate until the frosting sets, about 10 minutes. Cover the cake with the remaining frosting. For a very clean look, smooth the top and sides with an offset spatula or the straight edge of a bench scraper. Decorate the cake with raspberries, chocolate pearls, sprinkles, edible flowers, or candies. Evenly space 4 toothpicks into the top of the cake and loosely cover with plastic or reusable wrap (so the wrap doesn't touch the decorations) refrigerate for at least 1 hour before serving.

MAMI'S RUM CAKE
(BIZCOCHO DE RON)

From Von Diaz

For the Cake

Cooking spray

1 cup finely chopped walnuts

2 cups (240 grams) all-purpose flour

1 cup granulated sugar

1 (3.4-ounce) package instant vanilla pudding mix

1 stick unsalted butter, cut into small pieces

2 teaspoons baking powder

1 teaspoon fine salt

½ cup whole milk

4 large eggs

½ cup coconut oil, at room temperature (or warmed just until liquefied)

½ cup white or light rum

2 teaspoons pure vanilla extract

For the Rum Syrup

1 stick unsalted butter

½ cup white rum

½ cup lightly packed brown sugar

¼ cup water

½ teaspoon pure vanilla extract

This moist, rum-drenched cake is the perfect "tranquilizer" for tense election nights. It comes from food writer and radio producer Von Diaz. "My mother, who I call Mami, has always loved sweets and is a talented baker, capable of whipping up flan or cheesecake in what feels like minutes," writes Von. The rum glaze needs to settle into the cake for at least three hours or up to overnight, so plan ahead.

Position a rack in the center of the oven and preheat the oven to 325°F. Spray a 10-inch Bundt pan with cooking spray. Sprinkle the chopped walnuts over the bottom of the prepared pan.

Make the cake: In a stand mixer fitted with the paddle attachment (or in a large bowl using a handheld mixer), combine the flour, granulated sugar, pudding mix, butter, baking powder, and salt and beat on medium speed for 2 minutes. Add the milk, eggs, and oil and beat on low speed for 2 minutes more. Pour in the rum and vanilla and beat for 1 minute.

Pour the batter into the prepared pan and level the top with a rubber spatula. Bake for 50 to 60 minutes, until the cake is pale golden and slightly risen and a toothpick or cake skewer inserted into the center of the cake comes out clean. Let cool slightly in the pan on a wire rack.

Meanwhile, make the rum syrup: In a small saucepan, combine the butter, rum, sugar, water, and vanilla and bring to a boil over high heat, whisking to dissolve the sugar. Reduce the heat to medium-low and simmer until thickened slightly, 5 to 7 minutes.

While the cake is still warm, use a toothpick or skewer to poke deep holes all over the cake. Slowly pour the warm syrup evenly over the cake. Don't worry if it isn't absorbed immediately; it takes at least 10 minutes. Cover the pan with aluminum foil (or a plate) and let soak for at least 3 hours, or preferably overnight.

Invert the cake onto a plate and serve.

FUCK YOU, CAKE.

(P.S. I ACTUALLY LOVE YOU)

By VON DIAZ

For a long time, cake was my enemy.

But that wasn't always the case. As a kid I passionately gobbled up every sugary thing, and was fortunate to have a mother with an equally insatiable sweet tooth. She baked all the time, often from boxed cake mixes because they were quick and the best we could afford. Some of my fondest, earliest memories are of being in the kitchen with my mom, which often ended in her chasing me out with a wooden spoon in hand because I had stolen a spoonful (or two) of condensed milk meant for a flan.

But that all changed when puberty hit. My hips, stomach, and bust seemed to balloon overnight, and my family took to calling me *gordita*, or "chubby." Don't get me wrong, I was never a skinny kid. I've always been thick. Over the years my love of food and dexterity in the kitchen have contributed to a consistently ample waistline. As my partner often says, lovingly, there's not a straight line on me.

I was held to unrealistic beauty standards by both the men and women in my life. Never mind that traditional Puerto Rican and Southern foods—the cuisines of my two homes—are incredibly rich and fattening. Never mind that Caribbean women often have thick bellies and thighs. Never mind that family income dictates access to healthy, nutritious food. *You* are the problem, not society or culture. And these messages seeped into my subconscious in ways I'm only now starting to fully comprehend.

I first developed an eating disorder at age fifteen, which I struggled with well into my twenties. But by the time I developed a healthier relationship with eating, I had become convinced that cake was out to get me.

So I turned my back on dessert. I'd see those same irresistible cans of condensed milk from my childhood at the grocery store, and run away as if I'd spotted an ex-lover. Looking back, I can hear myself declining desserts at restaurants and people's homes, saying, "No, no, no. I have a salt tooth, not a sweet tooth." Or a simpler, "I don't care for sweets."

But that's a lie. Like so many other women I know, I've been dieting since adolescence. I still avoid all sorts of delicious things, at times watching my male counterparts inhale a huge slice of pie while I sit by feigning disinterest. The most alarming part of this dynamic in retrospect is that I came to believe that I had just outgrown dessert. That I truly didn't like it.

All too often, it's my instinct to hold up a mirror when something goes wrong. I blame myself for everything. Over the years, as I failed at every attempt to control what I ate, to avoid so many delicious things in the service of looking more like the women onscreen or in magazines, I was at fault. At times I felt betrayed by my adventurous palate, wishing, even praying that I could be satisfied by eating only "healthy" foods, and that I could find a way to eat less and less. Or maybe, hopefully, someday I could find a way to not want to eat at all.

I've witnessed this same internalized brutality in so many others. In my early career I worked as an advocate for women's rights, first with women and children at a domestic violence shelter and a rape crisis center, and later with an organization that helped women run for public office. In those worlds, and in my more recent work as a journalist and food writer, women have shared similar stories of self-hate. Today, I'm hard-pressed to call up a woman in my life who isn't actively watching what she eats, or fixated on the shape of her body.

Lately, I've been turning my anger outward. Each time I feel myself reach for that mirror that so clearly illuminates what's wrong with me, I release my grip and instead look with scrutiny at the systems that keep women in bondage. Because for much too long, my anger was misplaced. I know now that my love of food is *not* my enemy.

I wish I could tell you that I'm done hating cake. I'm not, but I'm working on it. In the meantime, I will eat in a way that nourishes me, and I'll keep baking the cakes my mom taught me (see my Mami's Rum Cake on page 103), and sharing big, buttery slices with as many people as I can.

PINEAPPLE UPSIDE-DOWN SPICE CAKE

From Kathy Gunst

For the Pineapple

1 small fresh pineapple
(2 to 2½ pounds)

½ stick unsalted butter

¾ cup packed light brown sugar

For the Cake

1¾ cups (210 grams) all-purpose flour

2 teaspoons baking powder

1½ teaspoons ground cardamom

1 teaspoon ground ginger

⅛ teaspoon ground allspice

Pinch of fine salt

1 stick unsalted butter,
at room temperature

1 cup granulated sugar

2 large eggs

½ teaspoon pure vanilla extract

½ cup fresh orange juice
(from about 1½ oranges)

The world is upside down and inside out and sometimes we just need a new way of looking at things. That's the intent behind this upside-down cake (and the fabulous Im-peach-ment Upside-Down Cake from Virginia Willis on page 108). It requires very little work or time—the whole thing is made in a cast-iron skillet—and is perfect for any time of year when pineapples are ripe and juicy. Thin slices of fresh pineapple are laid into the bottom of the skillet in caramelized brown sugar and butter and then a simple spice-infused cake batter is poured on top. Pop it in the oven, bake for just over a half hour, flip it out of the skillet, and you have an impressive dessert with a pineapple crown.

Position a rack in the center of the oven and preheat the oven to 375°F.

Prepare the pineapple: Trim the tough outer skin and any eyes off the outside of the pineapple. Cut the pineapple in half lengthwise and cut out the core with a small, sharp knife. Slice both halves crosswise into ½-inch-thick half-moons. You should have 18 to 20 slices.

In a 10-inch cast-iron or other heavy skillet, melt the butter over low heat. Increase the heat to medium, add the brown sugar, stir, and cook, stirring for 3 to 5 minutes, until the mixture is bubbling. Remove from the heat.

Carefully lay the pineapple slices on top of the brown sugar mixture, fitting the pieces together like a puzzle and pressing them down to create a flat layer. You may have more than one layer—fit the pineapple into the pan as tightly as possible.

continued

Make the cake: In a medium bowl, whisk together the flour, baking powder, cardamom, ginger, allspice, and salt.

In a stand mixer fitted with the paddle attachment, beat the butter on medium speed until soft and light, 2 to 3 minutes. Beat in the granulated sugar until light and fluffy, about 4 minutes more. Add the eggs one at a time, beating until each is fully incorporated before adding the next and stopping to scrape down the sides of the bowl as needed. Mix in the vanilla. Add half the flour mixture and beat on low speed until incorporated. Add the orange juice, beat to combine, and then the remaining flour mixture, mixing until just combined.

Pour the batter into the skillet over the pineapple and spread it evenly with a rubber spatula.

Bake until a toothpick inserted into the center of the cake comes out clean (try not to go all the way through to the pineapple), 30 to 40 minutes. Let cool in the skillet for about 5 minutes, but not too much longer or it may stick to the skillet. Place a large serving plate on top of the skillet and very carefully invert the skillet and plate together to flip the cake out onto the plate. Let cool slightly, then serve warm or at room temperature.

IM-PEACH-MENT UPSIDE-DOWN CAKE

From Virginia Willis

4 medium ripe peaches
(about 1½ pounds), unpeeled, pitted,
and cut into ⅓-inch-thick wedges

Juice of 1 lemon

1 cup (120 grams) cake flour

¾ teaspoon baking powder

¼ teaspoon baking soda

1 cup sugar

1 stick plus 2 tablespoons unsalted
butter, at room temperature

1 vanilla bean, split lengthwise and
seeds scraped, or 1 teaspoon pure
vanilla extract

2 large eggs

½ cup sour cream

Whipped cream, for serving

Cookbook author and activist Virginia Willis lives in Georgia and thinks Southern peaches are something special. "The trouble is," she writes, "you pretty much have to live in the South to understand what the fuss is all about. Upside-down cake is a Southern classic and is most often made with canned pineapple. This version uses fresh peaches and is a vast improvement, in my opinion. You can use all-purpose flour instead of the cake flour, but the results will be a bit heavier and slightly dense." A dollop of whipped cream on top of this cake sure doesn't hurt.

Position a rack in the center of the oven and preheat the oven to 350°F. Line an 18 x 13-inch rimmed baking sheet with a silicone baking mat or parchment paper.

Toss the peaches with the lemon juice in a large bowl. In a medium bowl, whisk together the flour, baking powder, and baking soda.

In a 10-inch cast-iron skillet, cook ¼ cup of the sugar over medium heat, stirring occasionally with a wooden spoon, for 5 to 8 minutes, until the sugar melts and turns deep amber. Remove from the heat. Immediately add the 2 tablespoons butter and stir vigorously to combine. Arrange the peach wedges in concentric circles over the sugar mixture, overlapping them as needed.

In a stand mixer fitted with the paddle attachment, combine the remaining ¾ cup sugar, the 1 stick butter, and the vanilla and beat on medium speed until smooth. Add the eggs one at a time, beating until each is fully incorporated before adding the next. Add the sour cream and beat until blended, stopping to scrape down the sides of the bowl as needed. With the mixer on low speed, gradually add the flour mixture and beat until combined, scraping the bowl as needed. Spoon the batter over the peaches in the skillet and spread with a spatula to cover evenly.

Place the skillet on the prepared baking sheet. Bake until the cake is golden brown and a toothpick inserted into the center comes out clean, 40 to 45 minutes. Let cool in the skillet on a wire rack for 10 minutes.

continued

Run a knife around the edge to loosen. Carefully pour any excess liquid from the skillet into a measuring cup and set aside. (It's okay if you don't have any excess liquid—it all depends on how fresh and juicy your peaches are.) Place a large serving plate on top of the skillet and very carefully invert the skillet and plate together to flip the cake out onto the plate. Drizzle the cake with the reserved liquid and let cool slightly, about 10 minutes. Cut into wedges using a serrated knife. Top with whipped cream and serve immediately.

LEMON CREAM CHEESE "POUND" CAKE

MAKES ONE 10-INCH BUNDT CAKE;

SERVES 8 TO 10

From Elle Simone Scott

For the Cake

3 cups (360 grams) cake flour,
plus more for dusting

3 cups sugar

1½ teaspoons baking powder

1 teaspoon fine salt

2 teaspoons finely grated lemon zest
(from about 2 lemons)

8 ounces cream cheese,
at room temperature

3 sticks unsalted butter, quartered,
at room temperature, plus more
for buttering

1½ teaspoons vanilla bean paste or
pure vanilla extract

6 large eggs, at room temperature,
lightly beaten

2 tablespoons fresh lemon juice

For the Glaze

1½ cups confectioners' sugar

1 teaspoon finely grated lemon zest

2 tablespoons fresh lemon juice

1 tablespoon buttermilk

When Elle Simone Scott, of PBS's America's Test Kitchen *as well as culinary mentor and activist, sent us this cake it quickly became a favorite. Her poem, in honor of her great-grandmother, reminded us of the power of women's voices and that a cake is more than flour, butter, and sugar.*

Position a rack in the center of the oven and preheat the oven to 325°F. Generously brush a 10-inch Bundt pan with butter and dust the bottom and sides with flour until well coated, then tap out any excess.

Make the cake: Sift the flour, sugar, baking powder, and salt into a large bowl. Mix in the lemon zest with a fork, breaking up any clumps.

In a stand mixer fitted with the paddle attachment, combine the cream cheese, butter, and vanilla and beat on medium-high speed until smooth and slightly airy, 2 to 3 minutes, stopping to scrape down the sides of the bowl as needed. Add half the eggs (it may look a little curdled at first, but keep beating), then add the remaining eggs and the lemon juice and beat until well combined and smooth, scraping down the sides of the bowl as needed.

With the mixer on low speed, add the flour mixture in three batches, gently beating until just combined after each addition, scraping down the sides as needed. Pour the batter into the prepared pan and smooth the top using an offset spatula. To release air bubbles, gently tap the pan on the counter.

Bake until the cake is golden brown and a toothpick inserted into the center comes out clean or with a few crumbs attached, about 1 hour 15 minutes. Let cool in the pan on a wire rack for 15 minutes. Place a plate over the top of the pan and carefully invert the plate and pan together to turn the cake out onto the plate. Lift the pan and let cool for up to 2 hours.

Meanwhile, make the glaze: In a small bowl, whisk together all the glaze ingredients until evenly combined.

Drizzle the glaze over the cooled cake and let sit for 15 minutes before serving.

Mother Dear

By
ELLE
SIMONE
SCOTT

Ann.

Mississippi morning, sunrises bore burning crosses and separate lives.

Mother Dear put her babies on that train North. Dressed in Sabbath best.

Shoebox of Chicken. Lemon Pound Cake.

And notes to Mama & Cousin:

"Take care of my babies.

Margie will be yo' kitchen help.

George will enlist soon.

Edith will need hugs but CAN pick the collards.

I'll be heading North whether husban' comes or not.

See ya'll soon, Annie."

First winter North. Crowda' peas boil, windows steaming.

Detroit. Black Bottom. Wrong side of the tracks—life.

Gospel: Mahalia, Leontyne: Opera.

Xmas, pine tree aroma and Mother Dear's train has entered the station.

Annie here, gifts from South. Quilts with names, family albums,

Coconut Cake, Mama's dinner rolls and Lemon Pound Cake.

ROOT BEER CAKE
with **CHOCOLATE-ROOT BEER GLAZE**

From Carla Hall

For the Cake

Cooking spray (optional)

2¼ cups (270 grams) all-purpose flour

1½ cups granulated sugar

½ cup lightly packed brown sugar

1 teaspoon baking soda

1 teaspoon smoked or
regular ground cinnamon

1 teaspoon freshly grated nutmeg

1 teaspoon ground star anise

½ teaspoon fine salt

1½ cups (12 ounces) root beer

2 sticks unsalted butter,
plus more for buttering if needed

¼ cup unsweetened natural cocoa
powder (not Dutch-process)

2 large eggs

½ cup buttermilk

1 teaspoon pure vanilla extract

1 teaspoon grated peeled fresh ginger

For the Glaze

¼ cup root beer, plus up to 1 tablespoon
more if needed

½ stick unsalted butter

1½ tablespoons unsweetened
natural cocoa powder

8 ounces (2 cups) confectioners'
sugar, sifted

⅛ teaspoon freshly grated nutmeg

⅛ teaspoon ground star anise

¼ teaspoon fine salt

"This cake is inspired by one for a Coca-Cola cake that I found on one of my grandmother's recipe cards," writes chef, author, and TV personality Carla Hall. *"This version is an homage to her, but amped up with the spicy flavors of root beer. If there's one thing that I learned growing up around a lot of strong Southern women, it's that our determination leads to results, and we need to celebrate each victory along the way, however small it may seem in the moment. Reward yourself with a piece of cake, then, once you're fortified, get out there again."*

If you serve the cake with a scoop of vanilla ice cream, it tastes like a deconstructed root beer float.

Position a rack in the center of the oven and preheat the oven to 350°F. Mist a 10-cup Bundt pan with cooking spray or brush with butter.

Make the cake: In a large bowl, whisk together the flour, both sugars, the baking soda, cinnamon, nutmeg, star anise, and salt until evenly combined.

In a small saucepan, combine the root beer, butter, and cocoa powder and bring to a boil, stirring occasionally, until the butter has melted. Let cool.

In a small bowl, whisk together the eggs, buttermilk, vanilla, and ginger. Add the buttermilk mixture to the flour mixture and stir until all the flour is moistened. Stir in the cooled root beer mixture until just combined to make a loose batter.

Scrape the batter into the prepared pan. Bake until a toothpick inserted into the center of the cake comes out clean and the cake pulls away from the side of the pan, 50 to 55 minutes. Let cool in the pan on a wire rack for 15 minutes. Invert the cake onto the rack and let cool until just slightly warm.

Meanwhile, make the glaze: Bring the root beer to a boil in a small saucepan, then stir in the butter and cocoa powder until completely smooth. Pour the root beer mixture into a medium bowl, then whisk in the confectioners' sugar, nutmeg, star anise, and salt until smooth and glossy.

continued

Set the warm cake on the rack over a bowl or rimmed baking sheet to catch any glaze. Pour the glaze over the top of the cake, allowing it to drip down the sides. Let the glaze set, about 10 minutes. Serve warm or at room temperature. The cake can be stored, covered, at room temperature for up to 3 days.

MARBLED CRANBERRY CHEESECAKE

From Kathy Gunst

For the Crust

12 whole graham crackers (8 x 5 inches)

5 tablespoons unsalted butter, melted, plus more for buttering

¼ cup sugar

Pinch of fine salt

For the Cranberry Puree

12 ounces frozen cranberries (no need to thaw)

¾ cup water

⅓ cup sugar

1 teaspoons pure vanilla extract

Finely grated zest of 1 orange

For the Cheesecake Batter

24 ounces cream cheese, at room temperature

1 cup whole-milk ricotta cheese

1 cup sugar

4 large eggs, at room temperature

1½ teaspoons pure vanilla extract

2 cups sour cream

For many years this rich, luscious cheesecake graced our Thanksgiving dessert table. It's truly a cake to give thanks for and one that need not wait for a holiday. The crust is made from ground graham crackers, topped with a batter of cream cheese, ricotta, and sour cream. A puree of cranberries is swirled into the batter (think of marbled Italian paper). The tart cranberries (with a hint of orange zest) provide a great counterpoint to the creamy richness of the cake.

The cake is baked for an hour at low heat and then kept in the warm oven for another hour. This method avoids the need for a water bath (a traditional method) and avoids the dreaded crack in the cheesecake. This cake is best made a day ahead, as it needs to chill for at least eight hours.

Position a rack in the center of the oven and preheat the oven to 350°F. Butter a 9 x 2¾-inch springform pan.

Make the crust: Process the graham crackers in a food processor until finely ground; you should have 1½ cups. Add the melted butter, sugar, and salt and pulse to combine. Transfer the graham cracker mixture to the prepared pan, pressing it evenly over the bottom and about 1 inch up the sides of the pan. Bake until set, 12 to 14 minutes. Set the pan on a wire rack and let cool thoroughly. Reduce the oven temperature to 275°F.

Make the cranberry puree: In a medium saucepan, combine the cranberries and water and bring to a boil over high heat. Reduce the heat to medium-low and simmer for 5 minutes. Stir in the sugar and cook for 3 to 5 minutes more, until the cranberries have burst and thickened. Transfer the mixture to a fine-mesh sieve set over a medium bowl and, using a rubber spatula, push the cranberries through; discard the solids in the sieve. Stir the vanilla and orange zest into the cranberry puree and let cool completely.

continued

Make the cheesecake batter: In a stand mixer fitted with the paddle attachment, combine the cream cheese, ricotta, and sugar and beat on low speed until fully blended and softened, about 1 minute. Add the eggs one at a time, beating until each is fully incorporated before adding the next. Add the vanilla and sour cream and beat until smooth, stopping to scrape down the sides of the bowl and the paddle as needed.

Spoon *half* the batter into the pan. Drop *half* the cranberry puree in spoonfuls on top of the batter in a random pattern. Using a table knife, swirl the cranberry puree through the batter in a swirly pattern (swirling horizontally and then vertically); do not overmix. Top with the remaining batter and then the remaining cranberry puree, again dropping it in spoonfuls in a random pattern, and again swirling the cranberry puree with a knife through the batter. It should look like Italian marbled paper.

Place the cake on a baking sheet and bake for 1 hour. Turn the oven off and leave the cake in the warm oven for another hour, then transfer to a wire rack and let cool to room temperature (the center will still be a bit wobbly when you remove it from the oven, but it will firm up as it cools). Cover and refrigerate for at least 8 hours or up to overnight.

To serve, run a knife under hot tap water, then dry, and run the knife around the edge of the pan and remove the springform ring. When ready to cut, warm and dry the knife again and cut the cheesecake.

4

COMFORT WITH A HELPING OF
Righteous Rage:
PUDDINGS AND CUSTARDS

RECIPE LIST

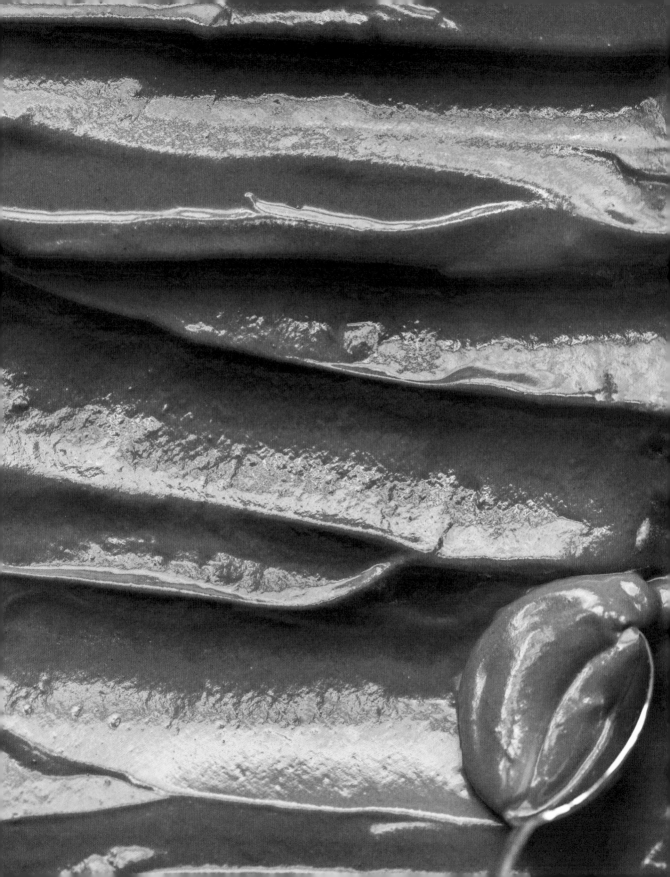

CHOCOLATE PUDDING NOW

From Alice Medrich

2 tablespoons cornstarch

⅛ teaspoon fine salt

2¼ cups whole milk (or 2 cups milk and ¼ cup heavy cream, if you like)

1 cup (about 6 ounces) semisweet (or dark or extra-dark) chocolate chips, preferably 60% cacao

Whipped cream, for serving (optional)

"Sometimes, chocolate pudding is just what's needed," says chocolate expert and cookbook author Alice Medrich. "When you—or the people you love—need satisfaction, or comfort, or control over something, try chocolate pudding. This recipe is as easy as it gets with results infinitely better than anything made from a box. I have fancier recipes that call for fancier chocolate, but this one does the job impressively (and immediately), with three ingredients you probably have on hand." We couldn't have said it better. Try it. You won't be sorry.

Have a timer, heatproof spatula, and six 1-cup custard cups or ramekins near the stove. In a medium saucepan, combine the cornstarch, salt, milk, and chocolate. Cook over medium heat, whisking continuously and scraping the bottom, sides, and corners of the pan, until the chocolate has melted and the first bubbles appear around the edges, 8 to 9 minutes. Simmer gently, whisking and scraping the pan continuously as the pudding thickens, 2 minutes more, adjusting the heat as necessary to prevent it from boiling furiously.

Immediately scrape the pudding into the custard cups or ramekins. If desired, top with whipped cream before serving. Serve warm, or at room temperature, or cold (my favorite). If you don't like the skin that forms on pudding, you can press plastic or reusable wrap against the surface. Refrigerate for up to 2 days.

THREE-CITRUS FLAN
with **MAKRUT LIME**

From Amy Besa

2½ cups whole milk

1 cup heavy cream

1½ cups sugar

4 wide strips lime zest

4 wide strips orange zest

4 wide strips lemon zest

6 to 8 fresh or dried makrut lime leaves

Pinch of fine salt

¼ cup water

3 large eggs

4 large egg yolks

Caramel Tips

Making caramel can be intimidating. But if you remember to swirl, not stir, and stop cooking the sugar before it is golden brown, it is easier to manage. Hardened sugar and caramel can be tough to remove, but here's a tip for easy cleanup: Once the sugar is out of the pot, fill the pot with water and bring it to a boil, then let sit until cool, and cleanup is not a problem.

Amy and her husband, Chef Romi Dorotan, own the pioneering Filipino restaurant Purple Yam in Brooklyn, New York. Amy is a powerhouse—an ambassador for Filipino food and culture. This take on flan brings the bright flavors of the Philippines together with classic caramel custard.

Makrut lime leaves are often sold as kaffir lime leaves. However, "kaffir" is a racist word meaning nonbeliever or infidel, and it's not okay to use. These leaves can be found in Thai and Asian food markets (see Mail-Order Rage on page 163).

Position a rack in the center of the oven and preheat the oven to 325°F.

In a medium saucepan, mix together the milk, cream, ½ cup of the sugar, the citrus zests, lime leaves, and salt. Heat over medium heat until the mixture just comes to a simmer, 6 to 8 minutes. Remove from the heat and let steep, uncovered, for 15 minutes.

In a heavy-bottomed medium saucepan, combine the remaining 1 cup sugar and the water. Bring to a boil over high heat, then reduce the heat to medium so the sugar simmers gently and cook, *without stirring*, but swirl the pan until the sugar is a golden caramel, about 10 minutes. Pour the caramel into a 4- to 6-cup au gratin dish or an 8-inch deep-dish pie pan, carefully tilt the dish to coat evenly. Place the caramel-coated dish in a large baking pan.

Lightly whisk the eggs and egg yolks in a medium bowl. While whisking, slowly pour the milk mixture into the eggs. Strain through a fine-mesh sieve into the caramel-coated dish; discard the lime zest and leaves.

Carefully transfer the baking pan to the oven. Pour hot water into the pan to reach two-thirds up the sides of the baking dish. Loosely lay a piece of aluminum foil over the flan. Bake until set around the edges but still slightly jiggly in the center, about 55 minutes.

Carefully transfer the baking dish to a wire rack to cool. Cover and refrigerate for 2 hours or up to overnight.

To serve, run a knife around the edges of the flan, place a serving plate on top, and invert it onto the plate with all the juicy caramel.

RAGE

By **JESSICA B. HARRIS**

If you would like to make a payment, press 1. To inquire about new products, press 2. For information about billing questions, press 3!"

I can feel the headache beginning as the "soothing" music plays. The list drones on until I finally get to my goal: "To speak with a representative, press *6." I do, and am informed that all representatives are currently busy and there will be a wait time of fifteen minutes or more. I wait relatively patiently, and just as I am about to be connected . . . *click*, a dial tone, and I'm back to my starting point. Now I'm vibrating with anger, two minutes away from screaming curses at a recording, with my blood pressure spiking dangerously and temples throbbing. Yup . . . it's rage with a capital R. Teeth-gnashing, stroke-producing, full-tilt boogie RAGE!! When it hits, the way I often calm down is with some kitchen therapy.

I take myself into my daffodil-yellow sanctuary and find the tarnished silver and care-darkened copper, get out my tools and begin to scrub and rub. Soon the rhythmic motions of applying the polish, moving the cloth back and forth, rinsing, assessing the results help me to regain composure and calm. By the time the place settings and the *batterie de cuisine* are beginning to shine, I have returned to my real world and avoided the medical consequences of overassociation with the madness of twenty-first-century life.

My kitchen is a refuge from the vicissitudes of the modern world. Others may find solace in baking and in creating bread that allows for punching and dough that can be whacked. I find relief in the rhythmic strokes of smooth cloth on silver and of the meditatively repetitive back-and-forth of copper polish on cookware.

It's often more about copper than silver. The copper is always heavy and thick with verdigris from use, but each piece evokes a memory. There's the first crepe pan that was a gift from a girlfriend more than forty years ago, the copper wok that is used almost nightly, and the huge fish poacher that I got at Dean & DeLuca eons ago, on sale because it had a few dings. The silver, too, comes with memories, but they are more of family. I see my mother with the pink polish and the soft blue cloth sprucing up the good silver for a special dinner or shining up the ridiculously large tea service for the church's annual Palm Sunday tea. Entering my polishing reverie, I rub away. I do not end up with goodies to share with others, but the shining vessels that result always make me smile and more often than not move me to cook.

All in all, it's way better than Prozac.

CHERRY AND FIG CLAFOUTI

From Katherine Alford

2 tablespoons unsalted butter, plus more for buttering

1 pound cherries, pitted

6 fresh black or green figs, stems trimmed, halved

⅔ cup granulated sugar, plus more for dusting

⅓ cup cognac, brandy, or rum

3 large eggs

1 cup half-and-half or whole milk

¼ teaspoon pure almond extract

¼ teaspoon fine salt

⅓ cup (40 grams) cake flour

Confectioners' sugar, for dusting

Clafouti is a French seasonal-fruit dessert made with what is essentially a baked crepe batter. Cherries are the classic ingredient, but sautéed apples, pears, or macerated berries are equally delicious. A generous pour of brandy or liquor is also traditional. In early summer when figs and cherries are both in season, I can't resist a jubilee-like flambé before baking. I love these fruits for both their flavor and mythology. Cherries for fertility, beauty, and protection against evil. And it was under a fig tree where the Buddha found enlightenment. In these times, women need all the protection and light we can get.

Position a rack in the center of the oven and preheat the oven to 425°F. Lightly brush a 4- to 6-cup au gratin dish or an 8-inch deep-dish pie pan with butter and sprinkle with some sugar.

In a large skillet, melt the butter over medium-high heat. Add the cherries and figs to the skillet, stir in 2 tablespoons of the granulated sugar, and cook until bubbling, 2 to 3 minutes. Remove the skillet from the heat and pour in the cognac. Return to the heat and, if cooking over a gas flame, tip the skillet slightly to ignite the liquor. (Warning: It's going to flambé!) Cook until the flame subsides or the liquor has reduced by half, about 4 minutes. Set aside to cool slightly.

Whisk together the remaining granulated sugar, the eggs, half-and-half, almond extract, and salt, in a large bowl. Add the flour and whisk until well combined and smooth. (Alternatively, the batter can be prepared in a blender.)

Pour the fruit and any juices into the prepared dish, then top with the batter. Bake for 15 minutes, then reduce the oven temperature to 350°F and bake until set, puffy, and golden brown, about 25 minutes more. Let cool on a wire rack for 10 minutes. Dust with confectioners' sugar and serve warm.

AFTER THE HEARINGS

By PAM HOUSTON

I watched the Kavanaugh hearings surrounded by smart, soulful, sarcastic, and deep-hearted women. Writers who come to my Colorado ranch once a year to talk about art. As the hours passed we took turns holding hands, punching pillows; every now and then a sigh turned into a sob. When it was all over, after every one of those chinless men had at first believed the professor, after the frat boy's rage and bluster reminded them all the ways the truth was irrelevant, we picked ourselves up and walked to the river. The young Rio Grande—lowered significantly by the climate catastrophe it was getting more impossible for even the conservatives in the county to ignore—flowed past us. We looked into each other's faces, faces that seemed to have aged a decade in the five or six hours we had been in front of the TV. We would all be gone, before long, that seemed certain now, and the river would still flow, or some other river would, eventually, and that was all I could muster in the way of hope.

We went back to the house, back to the kitchen. We preheated the oven. We cut garlic and parsley and lemon for the marinade, peeled potatoes and carrots, unwrapped the roast from its brown waxed paper, cut half-moons into the fat and laid in slivers of garlic, ground the French salt with a mortar and pestle, tucked sprigs of rosemary under the white string, sank the thermometer into the thick of the meat. We tossed a salad of spinach, red onion, apples, and candied walnuts. We carved tiny x's in the foot of each Brussels sprout and put them on the stovetop to steam. In the living room, Sarna made Moscow Mules using the Fever-Tree ginger ale and all the limes the Kentucky Belle Market had after the weekend. Rowena folded sheets of colored paper into doves and put one on each dinner plate. Amanda went to the stereo, selected Mavis Staples: "*I know a place, ain't nobody cryin.*" The windows fogged and the smell of chimichurri filled the kitchen. Ten women, singing, dancing, feeding ourselves and each other. In spite of everything, we weren't dead yet.

MANGO-LIME-ORANGE CURD IN MERINGUE NESTS
(OR DON'T TELL ME WHAT TO DO WITH MY EGGS!)

From Kathy Gunst

For the Meringue Nests

¾ cup sugar

¾ cup egg whites (from about 6 large eggs)

⅛ teaspoon cream of tartar

Pinch of fine salt

½ teaspoon pure vanilla extract

For the Curd

2 cups mango cubes (about 1 large)

1 teaspoon lime zest

¼ cup fresh lime juice

½ teaspoon orange zest

¼ cup fresh orange juice

½ cup plus 2 tablespoons sugar

1 teaspoon pure vanilla extract

3 large egg yolks

1 large egg

1 stick unsalted butter, cut into 8 pieces and chilled

Meringues are egg whites in a frenzy. A good, crisp, shatter-in-your-mouth meringue is one of my favorite desserts. The trick is to make meringues on a day with very low humidity. The meringues are baked for two hours at 200°F, the oven is turned off, and the meringues are left to dry for another hour. If you bake them a day ahead, you can store them in the cooled oven (far away from any humidity) or in an airtight container.

You can get fancy and pipe the meringue out with a pastry bag, but I like to plop them onto a cookie sheet to give them a rustic look. Use the back of a kitchen spoon to make a small indentation in the center, ideal for filling with whipped cream and berries, but the mango-lime-orange curd is irresistible.

Curd is a topping or preserve made from citrus, butter, eggs, and sugar. Traditionally it is made from lemons, but I had a ripe mango on hand and a bunch of limes and an orange and thought, Why not? *As soon as I filled the meringue nests with the curd, I realized they looked exactly like fresh eggs, thus the alternate title.*

You may not need all the curd to fill the meringue nests, but you won't be the least bit unhappy to have a bunch of this tart-sweet curd left over. Spread it on morning toast or serve it on top of yogurt with fresh fruit, or with pound cake, lemon cake, cookies, or muffins.

Position racks in the center and upper third of the oven and preheat the oven to 350°F. Line two cookie sheets with parchment paper or silicone baking mats.

Spread the sugar over another baking sheet and bake on the center rack for 10 minutes.

Make the meringue nests: In a stand mixer fitted with the whisk attachment, combine the egg whites and cream of tartar and whisk on high speed until frothy, about 2 minutes.

continued

MANGO-LIME-ORANGE
CURD IN MERINGUE NESTS
(continued)

Remove the sugar from the oven and reduce the oven temperature to 200°F. *Very slowly* spoon the warm sugar into the egg whites, adding it bit by bit. When all the sugar is added, add the salt and vanilla and beat until the egg whites hold stiff peaks. When you lift the whisk out of the bowl, the egg whites should stand up straight, without slumping or flopping over.

Use a ⅓-cup dry measuring cup to scoop the meringue into 14 small mounds on the prepared pans, distributing them between the two pans. (Or you can transfer the meringue to a pastry bag, or make an impromptu pastry bag with a large resealable plastic bag—see page 99—and pipe it onto the prepared pans). Using the back of a soup spoon, create a small indentation in the middle of each mound (this is where the filling will go).

Bake for 2 hours, switching the sheets from top to bottom and bottom to top after 1 hour. If the meringues begin to brown, very loosely cover them with aluminum foil. Turn the oven off, but leave the meringues in the oven for another hour to crisp up. Store the meringues in the turned off oven or in an airtight container for up to 1 day.

Make the curd: In a blender or food processor, combine the mango, lime zest, lime juice, orange zest, and orange juice and puree until smooth. Pour the puree into a medium saucepan, add the ½ cup sugar and the vanilla, and bring to a gentle simmer over medium-low heat, stirring, until slightly thickened, about 5 minutes; take care not to let the mixture boil. Remove from the heat.

Meanwhile, whisk together the egg yolks, egg, and the 2 tablespoons sugar in a medium bowl. While whisking, slowly pour half the egg mixture into the warm fruit mixture and whisk until fully incorporated, then whisk in the remaining egg mixture. Cook over medium-low heat, whisking continuously, until the curd thickens, 6 to 8 minutes. Be careful *not to let the curd boil*. Remove from the heat and whisk in the butter one or two pieces at a time, stirring until each piece is melted and fully incorporated before adding the next.

Strain the curd through a fine-mesh sieve into a medium bowl, pressing it through with a rubber spatula; you should have about 3 cups. Press a piece of waxed paper or reusable wrap directly against the surface of the curd to prevent a skin from forming. Refrigerate until completely chilled, about 2 hours. (The curd will keep for about 4 days.)

Just before serving, fill the indentation in each meringue with some curd.

5

NO MORE
Humble Pie:
CRUMBLES, PIES, AND TARTS

RECIPE LIST

CHOCOLATE BANANA PUDDING PIE
with SALTED PEANUTS

From Katherine Alford

1 prepared chocolate or graham cracker crust

½ cup shredded coconut

1½ cups whole milk

3 large egg yolks

⅓ cup granulated sugar

¼ cup cornstarch

4 ounces semisweet chocolate, chopped

2 tablespoons unsalted butter

1 teaspoon pure vanilla extract

2 ripe bananas, pureed

½ cup heavy cream

2 tablespoons confectioners' sugar

⅓ cup salted peanuts, coarsely chopped, for garnish

Chocolate sprinkles, grated chocolate, or chocolate curls, for garnish

Something about chocolate, bananas, salted peanuts, and coconut evokes the fun and excess of the circus. And when the clowns in DC have turned our democracy into a three-ring circus, an over-the-top pie seems all too fitting. This is a sweet way to use ripe bananas instead of the familiar banana bread. Feel free to use a premade chocolate, graham cracker, or cookie crust, or even a homemade pretzel crust (see page 139) for a serious play on salty and sweet. Get creative with the toppings: more cookies, animal crackers, caramel corn, or sweet cereals all would fit the bill.

Position a rack in the center of the oven and preheat the oven to 350°F.

Bake the crust until golden brown or set, 12 to 15 minutes. Let cool. Spread the coconut on a small baking sheet and bake until lightly toasted, about 10 minutes. Let cool.

Heat the milk over medium-high heat in a medium saucepan until just before it boils; remove from the heat.

Whisk together the egg yolks and granulated sugar, in a medium bowl. Sift the cornstarch on top and mix. While whisking continuously, slowly pour the hot milk into the egg mixture and whisk until smooth. Return the mixture to the saucepan and cook over medium heat, whisking, until thickened and the mixture just starts to boil, about 5 minutes. Remove from the heat, add the chocolate, butter, and ½ teaspoon of the vanilla and whisk until the chocolate has melted and the mixture is well combined. Whisk in the pureed banana until combined.

Pour the pudding into the crust and press plastic wrap directly against the surface to prevent a skin from forming. Refrigerate until set, at *least* 2 hours.

When ready to serve, in a large bowl using a handheld mixer, whip the cream until it holds soft peaks. Add the confectioners' sugar and the remaining ½ teaspoon vanilla and whip until it holds semifirm but not grainy peaks.

Dollop the whipped cream over the pudding. Scatter the toasted coconut, peanuts, and chocolate over the top and serve.

A SUMMER DAY

This is the story of a day in Maine. It contains no mention of Himself, because He is all we ever talk about now, in these days of the Troubles. Instead, I hope you will allow me to celebrate a few small things, during this time when so much has been destroyed.

The night before, last thing before bed, I had mixed up some pizza dough. The recipe is pretty simple—all it really requires is flour, yeast, sea salt, and time.

This last ingredient is the one I never have.

The dough had been rising all night, and in the morning, on that first day of July, I divided it into a half dozen balls, dusted them with flour. These I covered with a tea towel, and let them rise again.

I made an omelet for my wife, Deedie, using some sausage and mushrooms and cheddar, and we ate it on the front porch, looking out on the waters of Long Pond, here in our village of Belgrade Lakes.

The week before, she and I had celebrated our thirtieth wedding anniversary.

By our feet the dogs looked up at us with their old, gray Labrador faces, hoping for a tidbit, and in this they were not completely disappointed.

After breakfast, we got in our little boat—the *Red Wedding*—and scudded across the lake to poke our heads in at the general store and also to visit the farmers' market. We startled a great blue heron. It rose unexpectedly from the reeds along the bank.

I had once told my daughter that she reminded me of that heron. "Sometimes you think you're too awkward, or too strange," I'd said. "But then you take wing."

It's okay if you want to roll your eyes at this. My daughter rolled her eyes, too.

At the farmers' market we bantered with the right-wing sausage man. Sometimes he wears a T-shirt that reads: "PETA: People Eating Tasty Animals." We also bought some garlic scapes, and some pesto, and some greens for salad.

Deedie and I headed back home and I tied the boat up at the dock. The dogs were howling piteously, unable to believe we hadn't included them on the boat ride.

The howling, however, had failed to wake my son, Sean. He was home after graduating college in May, spending the summer lolling around the lake house before heading on to graduate school in robotics in the fall.

When Sean finally woke up, we sat down together and watched soccer. I have loved spending time with him this summer. Sometimes I wish the games would go on forever.

IN MAINE

By JENNIFER FINNEY BOYLAN

It was hot for Maine—in the high eighties—and I spent part of the day swimming in the lake. Long Pond is full of rocks, and I banged my knee against one of them as I swam, and said, Ow. "Jenny," said my wife. "Are you okay?"

She'd been working in the garden. There she was, surrounded by elfin mountain laurel, Joe Pye weed, penstemon, masterwort, and vanilla gorilla.

I was fine. I took a walk down our dirt road. One of my neighbors passed me on an ATV. I tipped my straw hat to him as he went by.

In the afternoon my daughter and her girlfriend and three of her friends arrived, having driven up from Washington, DC, where it was considerably hotter. Bottles of ales were cracked open.

The young people hung around inside listening to The Decemberists while Deedie and I had gin and tonics on the porch. Then I tied on an apron and started up the pizza factory. I made six pies in all. One was a pie of capicola and mascarpone and fennel and red chili sauce, another featured the meat of one whole lobster that I'd steamed earlier and then simmered in red sauce.

For dessert we ate blueberry pie with ice cream.

I cleaned this all up as the young people headed out to the dock in the dark to swim. As I wiped down the counters, I listened to the new "lost" John Coltrane album, *Both Directions at Once*, which after fifty years on a shelf still sounds shocking and new.

Then my wife and I climbed into bed. Through the open windows we heard the calling of loons. They mate for life.

From the dock we heard the soft voices of our children and their friends. I could tell by Deedie's breath that she was already asleep. But I lay there for a while in the dark, listening to the sounds.

As I slowly drifted off, I thought of the closing lines of Manuel Puig's *Kiss of the Spider Woman*, when two lovers speak to each other through the strange haze of a dream.

"Oh how much I love you!" says one. "That was the only thing I couldn't tell you, I was so afraid . . . I was going to lose you forever."

"No, Valentin, beloved," comes the reply. "That will never take place, because this dream is short. But this dream is happy."

MAINE BLUEBERRY
SUPREME COURT CRUMBLE

From Kathy Gunst

For the Berries

3½ cups blueberries (or mixed berries)

1 tablespoon all-purpose flour

⅓ cup granulated sugar

1 teaspoon finely grated lemon zest

2½ tablespoons fresh lemon juice

¼ to ½ teaspoon ground ginger

Pinch of fine salt

For the Crumble Topping

⅔ cup (80 grams) all-purpose flour

⅔ cup your favorite granola

3 tablespoons granulated or
light brown sugar

Pinch of ground ginger

Pinch of fine salt

1 stick unsalted butter, cut into cubes
and chilled, plus room-temperature
butter for buttering

Whipped cream, vanilla ice cream,
or Greek-style yogurt (great for
breakfast), for serving

Let's just say that a certain senator from my home state of Maine let us all down in a big way. Let's just say that this senator—a so-called moderate Republican—pretended to listen to the women and men of her state and pretended to listen to the Kavanaugh hearings and pretended to stay open to voting until she had heard from Dr. Blasey Ford and Kavanaugh. Let's just say she crumbled. Badly.

This crumble is made with wild Maine blueberries, or any combination of raspberries, strawberries, blackberries, and blueberries. The crumble can be assembled and refrigerated up to a day ahead and baked just before serving.

Position a rack in the center of the oven and preheat the oven to 375°F. Lightly butter four 1-cup ramekins or a 9-inch pie plate.

Prepare the berries: In a large bowl, lightly toss the berries with the flour. Mix in the sugar, lemon zest, lemon juice, ginger, and salt. Divide the berries among the ramekins or put them in the pie plate.

Make the crumble topping: In a medium bowl, combine the flour, granola, sugar, ginger, and salt. Add the butter and, using your fingers or a pastry blender, work the butter into the flour mixture until it's the size of small pebbles.

Divide the crumble among the ramekins or sprinkle it over the fruit in the pie plate; gently press the topping down to form a crust.

Put the ramekins or pie plate on a baking sheet and bake until the topping turns golden brown and the fruit bubbles up at the sides, 20 to 35 minutes, depending on whether you're using ramekins or a pie plate.

Serve warm, topped with whipped cream, ice cream, or yogurt as desired.

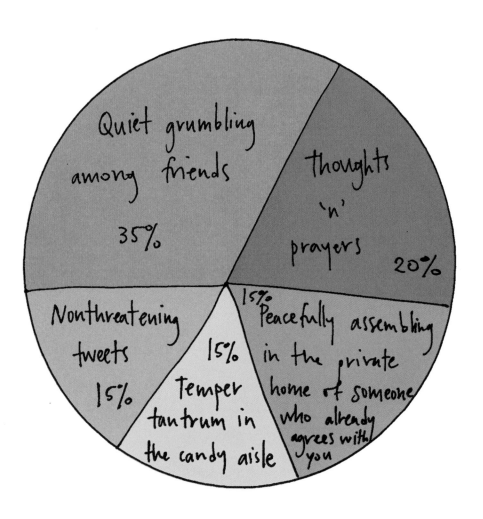

HOW WOULD THE ESTABLISHMENT LIKE YOU TO PROTEST?

Quiet grumbling among friends 35%

thoughts 'n' prayers 20%

Nonthreatening tweets 15%

15% Temper tantrum in the candy aisle

15% Peacefully assembling in the private home of someone who already agrees with you

ANN FRIEDMAN'S PIE CHART

BUTTERMILK PIE
with ORANGE MARMALADE AND PRETZEL CRUST

From Keia Mastrianni

For the Pretzel Crust

6 ounces salted mini pretzels

3 tablespoons sugar

1 stick plus 2 tablespoons unsalted butter, melted, plus more for buttering

For the Custard

¾ cup sugar

2 teaspoons all-purpose flour

½ teaspoon fine salt

1½ teaspoons finely grated lemon zest

3 tablespoons unsalted butter, melted

2 large eggs

1 large egg yolk

¾ teaspoon pure vanilla extract

1½ tablespoons sour cream

¾ cup buttermilk

¾ cup heavy cream

2 teaspoons fresh lemon juice

⅓ cup orange marmalade

"This pie is how I channel my sour-salty feelings into something more palatable. It's my metaphor for lemons into lemonade," writes Keia Mastrianni, a writer and baker at Milk Glass Pie in North Carolina. "A salty pretzel crust is layered with orange marmalade and a tangy buttermilk custard. The sweet-salty tang is a perfect complement to your next rage-fueled community supper. This is a pie that pairs well with activism."

Position a rack in the lower third of the oven and preheat the oven to 350°F. Lightly butter a 9-inch glass pie plate.

Make the pretzel crust: Put the pretzels in a food processor and pulse into fine crumbs. Add the sugar and pulse to incorporate. With the food processor running, stream in the melted butter and process until just combined.

Pour the pretzel mixture into the pie plate and, using your fingers or a metal measuring cup, press it over the bottom and up the sides. Freeze until solid, about 15 minutes.

Place the crust on a baking sheet and bake for 12 minutes, until the crust is fragrant and lightly browned. Let cool on the pan. Reduce the oven temperature to 325°F.

Meanwhile, make the custard: In a large bowl, combine the sugar, flour, and salt. Add the lemon zest and, using your fingers, rub it into the sugar mixture. Whisk in the melted butter. Whisk in the eggs and egg yolk one at a time, whisking until each is fully incorporated before adding the next. Whisk in the vanilla.

In a small bowl, whisk together the sour cream, buttermilk, and heavy cream, then stir in the lemon juice. Add the buttermilk mixture to the egg mixture and whisk together.

Use a rubber spatula to spread the orange marmalade over the bottom crust, leaving a 1-inch border uncovered. Pour the buttermilk custard into the crust. Bake for 30 minutes, then rotate the pie 180 degrees and bake for 15 to 20 minutes more, until the pie is golden brown along the edges and gently puffed up and set. Give it the jiggle test to make sure the center is fully cooked—it should jiggle like Jell-O, not wave like the ocean. Let cool completely before serving.

THREE-BERRY GALETTE

MAKES 1 GALETTE;
SERVES 6

From Kathy Gunst

For the Crust

1½ cups (180 grams) all-purpose flour, plus more for dusting

2 tablespoons sugar

Pinch of fine salt

1 stick unsalted butter, cut into small cubes and chilled

2 to 3 tablespoons ice water

1 tablespoon vodka

For the Fruit Filling

3 cups berries (1 cup each of raspberries, blueberries, and blackberries, but any berry or combo will work)

2 tablespoons sugar

1½ teaspoons all-purpose flour or cornstarch

1 teaspoon finely grated lemon zest

Pinch of fine salt

1 to 2 tablespoons heavy cream, for brushing (optional)

What I love most about a galette—also called a croustade or crostada—is how adaptable and simple to put together it is. In the summer I fill the buttery pastry with a mixture of berries, and in the fall I opt for thinly sliced apples and pears (see page 144). The pastry is rolled into a circle and filled with fruit, and then the edges of the pastry are draped in and over most of the fruit in a rustic, simple manner. Make the dough ahead of time and you can have this beautiful fruit galette on the table in about an hour.

Make the crust: In a food processor, pulse the flour, sugar, and salt to combine. Add the butter and pulse until the mixture resembles cornmeal with bean-size bits of butter. Combine 2 tablespoons water and the vodka and drizzle it over the flour mixture. Pulse until the dough just starts coming together but stop before it gathers into a ball. To see if the dough is moist enough, grab a handful of the dough and squeeze it; if it's crumbly, add 1 to 3 teaspoons of the remaining water. Form the dough into a disk, wrap it in parchment paper or reusable wrap, and chill for at least 1 hour or up to 2 days.

Let the dough come to room temperature for about 10 minutes. Line a baking sheet with parchment paper or a silicone baking mat.

On a lightly floured work surface, roll the dough into a 14-inch circle, and transfer it to the prepared pan. Refrigerate while you prepare the fruit.

Make the fruit filling: In a large bowl, gently mix the berries, sugar, flour, lemon zest, and salt.

Spoon the berry mixture into the center of the dough, leaving 2 to 3 inches from the edge. Fold the dough in over the fruit, leaving the fruit at the center exposed and pleating the dough as you work around the galette. Refrigerate for 15 to 20 minutes.

Position a rack in the center of the oven and preheat the oven to 400°F.

Bake the galette for 15 minutes. Remove from the oven and brush the crust with the cream, if using. Return to the oven, reduce the oven temperature to 350°F, and bake until the crust is golden brown and the fruit is bubbling, 20 to 30 minutes more.

Cool the galette on the baking sheet for 5 to 10 minutes. Serve warm or at room temperature.

APPLE-PEAR GALETTE

From Kathy Gunst

Dough (page 142)

2 tart apples

1 ripe pear, Bosc or other firm variety

1 teaspoon fresh lemon juice

1½ tablespoons apple cider

½ teaspoon ground cinnamon

½ teaspoon ground ginger

Pinch of ground allspice

2 tablespoons all-purpose flour

2 tablespoons sugar

1 tablespoon heavy cream, for brushing

Prepare the dough, roll it out, place on a baking sheet, and chill as directed on page 142.

Peel, core, and slice the apples and pear into ¼-inch slices. Toss in a large bowl with the lemon juice, cider, cinnamon, ginger, and allspice and set aside. Add the flour and sugar and toss again.

Pile the apples and pear into the center of the dough (or arrange them in concentric circles), leaving the outer 2 inches free of fruit. Fold the dough in toward the fruit, leaving the fruit at the center exposed and pleating the dough as you work around the galette. Refrigerate for 15 to 20 minutes.

Position a rack in the center of the oven and preheat the oven to 400°F.

Bake the galette for 15 minutes. Remove from the oven and brush the crust with the cream. Return to the oven, reduce the oven temperature to 350°F, and bake until the crust is golden brown and the fruit is bubbling, 30 to 40 minutes more.

Let the galette cool on the baking sheet for 5 to 10 minutes, then transfer to a serving plate. Serve warm or at room temperature.

PIE TIPS

*K*atherine spent five years teaching in a professional cooking school in New York City. "Without a doubt, the most fun class to teach was pie day," she says. "Many cooks have a serious 'fear of pieing.' But with a basic understanding of the elements that make up a good pie, students came away far more confident and assured."

A great tender, flaky pie crust is the result of beads of fat suspended in between layers of moistened flour. You'll notice we prefer butter for its taste (a lard crust is a revelation, but does freak some people out). Shortening is often called for in piecrust, and it can be easier to work with, but who really likes the taste of shortening? If you wouldn't spread it on toast or an ear of corn, why does it belong in your pie? That said, if you are making pie for the first time or have pie anxiety, no judgment if you substitute shortening for a quarter of the amount of butter called for in the recipe. Shortening is easier to work with because it has no water in it. Butter does. When flour is moistened with water, the proteins develop gluten, a weblike structure. In a successful crust, the nuggets of fat interrupt the gluten strands, hence "shortening" them, resulting in a tender, flaky, delicious crust. Crust needs *some* gluten; otherwise, it will crumble and won't hold together. However, overworked dough gets tough. If you follow some basic tenets, you can be confident working with an all-butter crust.

TEMPERATURE IS PROBABLY THE MOST IMPORTANT ELEMENT in making a piecrust. Always work with butter straight from the fridge. Cut it into ½-inch cubes. As noted, we love using a bench scraper for this. If the butter gets too warm while you are dicing it, return it to the fridge to solidify. It might seem like a great idea to work with frozen butter, but that creates crumbly doughs. Generally, we like to measure the butter first, cut it into cubes, and return it to the fridge while we're pulling the rest of the ingredients together. Flour should be measured accurately, but this is one instance in baking where you do have some wiggle room.

BY HAND OR FOOD PROCESSOR? It's up to you, because both methods can result in wonderful crusts. The advantage of a food processor is that it's fast and you are not in direct contact (meaning warming it with your body heat) with the butter. The advantage of a hand-made crust is that you're less likely to overwork it, have more control, and have the tactile satisfaction of working in the butter. And using a knife or a pie cutter, rather than a machine, means the butter doesn't get too warm.

ADDING BUTTER IN STAGES is a great way to coat the flour with fat before incorporating larger bits. In a food processor, add a quarter of the amount of butter (or shortening, if that's what you're using) and pulse until the flour is powdery and tinted yellow. Then add the remaining butter and pulse until it's broken down into pieces ranging in size from small peas to lima beans.

MOST PIE DOUGH CALLS FOR ICE WATER. Measure the water and then add 1 or 2 ice cubes. Add the water to the flour in stages (but not the ice cubes). It often may feel like the dough isn't wet enough, and you may be tempted to add more liquid. However, dough with too much liquid can get tough and shrink. But often it's more about even distribution of the liquid; the dough will hydrate during resting. With some of our crusts we add a touch of vodka (yes, vodka). This is a way to moisten the flour without water. The vodka doesn't stimulate gluten development, but does turn to steam when heated and can result in a light crust.

WHEN THE DOUGH IS TURNED OUT ONTO PLASTIC WRAP, it's very helpful to use the wrap to pull the loose parts of the dough together. Pressing the dough tightly in the wrap compacts it into a cohesive disk with smooth edges.

ALWAYS REST THE DOUGH IN THE FRIDGE before rolling it out. This lets the gluten relax, hydrates the flour evenly, and returns the butter to a solid state. Chilling dough for 1 hour is fine, but several hours, or up to overnight, is best. Well-rested doughs don't shrink as much as they bake.

PULL THE DOUGH OUT OF THE REFRIGERATOR ABOUT 10 MINUTES BEFORE ROLLING IT OUT.

LIGHTLY DUST YOUR WORK SURFACE WITH FLOUR. When Katherine was teaching, she watched experienced bakers throw flour effortlessly and evenly over the work surface. The trick is to think of throwing the flour like skipping a stone over the smooth surface of a pond. It should be a dusting, not a drowning. If you add too much flour, simply brush it off with a pastry brush.

TO GET THE DOUGH MALLEABLE enough for rolling, it's best to whack it with the rolling pin a couple of times to get it ready to roll. Also great for getting out that rage!

ROLL IN ONE DIRECTION from the center of the dough out to the edge. Take care to not roll over the edge, or the dough may stick to the counter. You can control the shape of the dough by adding a little more pressure on one end of the rolling pin. The dough should be free-moving and slip easily on the counter at all times; slipping a bench scraper or offset spatula underneath to loosen any stuck bits can help. It doesn't hurt to turn the dough over once as well. If the dough gets warm or pasty at any time, slip it onto an inverted baking pan and return it to the refrigerator to cool down. Don't rush it, and remember you are in charge! (Pie and life lessons go together.) If it's an exceedingly hot day, roll the dough between two pieces of parchment paper.

ONCE THE DOUGH IS ROLLED OUT to the specified shape, drape it over the rolling pin or fold into quarters to transfer to a pie plate. Don't stretch the dough into the pan, let it fall and drape easily.

FOLD THE DOUGH UNDER TO MAKE A DOUBLE THICKNESS at the rim of the pan. The easiest crimp is to press the tines of a fork along the edges of the dough. Another option is to make indentations with your fingers. With one hand on the inside of the crust use your index finger and thumb to create a "V." Press the dough into the V with the index finger of your other hand to make a fluted edge. Repeat around the crust. Chill.

RETURN THE CRUST TO THE REFRIGERATOR for 15 minutes to 1 hour before baking or blind baking (see below). Rolled crusts can also be wrapped frozen for up to 2 months.

DOUBLE DUTY: PIE DOUGH RECIPES ARE EASY TO DOUBLE and freeze (double wrapped). Frozen dough is great to have on hand when you want to pull a pie together in no time. Thaw at room temperature or in the fridge for a day if you have that luxury of time.

ONE OF THE MOST COMMON PIE MISTAKES IS UNDERBAKING. In an underbaked crust, the texture will be doughy, not crisp, and the flavors won't be fully developed. To avoid this, we often prebake a crust before filling (aka blind baking). Blind baking ensures that a crust with a filling will be fully cooked. Line the crust with aluminum foil or parchment paper and fill with dried beans, rice, or reusable pie weights. These weights ensure the crust holds it shape. (We keep old beans or rice around specifically for this use. They can be reused several times for blind baking.) Baking times vary depending on the type of crust, but when the crust is set remove the weights or beans, and if indicated return the crust to the oven to finish baking. In the final crust a couple of dark spots are a-okay with us. A reusable plastic or metal pie shield is a handy piece of equipment if you make a lot of pie. It protects the crust from overbaking while the filling bakes, but you can fashion one by folding a piece of foil and tucking it around and over the exposed crust.

ALWAYS LET THE PIE COOL before slicing. Warm pie is delicious, but hot pie can be a runny fail. Patience is a virtue.

WE ALSO WANT TO POINT OUT that premade crusts—which have improved vastly over the past few years—can be a great time-saver. No judgment here. Look for brands that use real ingredients and no preservatives. Keep in mind that frozen crusts in tins are often slightly smaller than a traditional 9-inch pie, so you may have excess filling.

PIE IS A LIFELONG PROCESS. ONE THAT GETS **BETTER EVERY TIME.**

BROWN BUTTER
VINEGAR PIE

From Katherine Alford

Dough (page 142) or premade crust

1 stick unsalted butter

4 large eggs

2 tablespoons apple cider vinegar

¾ cup granulated sugar

½ cup packed light or dark brown sugar

½ teaspoon ground cinnamon or allspice

1½ teaspoons pure vanilla extract

Pinch of fine salt

I first tasted vinegar pie at Pie for Breakfast, a wonderful restaurant in Pittsburgh. Although I was initially suspicious (vinegar pie?), I immediately fell for it. I, too, have been told that I am too tart and acidic. Vinegar pie also comes with a great backstory.

Vinegar pie is in a class of desserts known as "desperation" pies made by Appalachian women during the Depression. Lemons were both scarce and expensive, so bakers substituted vinegar. Browning the butter for this pie adds a nutty richness that stands up to the vinegar. Although we include a crust recipe, no judgment if you use a premade one. This will satisfy a craving for pie when there isn't much in the house. Once again, women figuring out how to make do and make the best of things in tough times.

Prepare the dough as directed on page 142.

Preheat the oven to 425°F.

On a lightly floured surface, roll the dough into a 13-inch round. Ease it into a 9-inch pie plate; crimp the edges as desired. Freeze until firm, about 15 minutes.

Line the crust with a piece of parchment paper or aluminum foil and fill it with about 1½ cups dried beans, rice, or pie weights. Bake until the edges are just set and golden brown, 12 to 15 minutes. Remove the parchment and weights and return the crust to the oven. Bake until the bottom of the crust sets and gets a little color, about 7 minutes more. Remove the piecrust and reduce the oven temperature to 325°F.

Meanwhile, make the filling: Melt the butter in a medium saucepan over medium heat, then cook, swirling the pan, until it smells toasted and nutty, about 7 minutes. Set aside to cool slightly.

In a medium bowl, whisk together the eggs, vinegar, granulated sugar, brown sugar, cinnamon, vanilla, and salt. Whisk in the browned butter until smooth. Pour the mixture into the crust. Bake the pie until the filling is set and the edges are slightly puffed, 25 to 30 minutes. Let cool on a wire rack for up to 1 hour before serving.

From **IF DESSERT BE FRAGILE SKY**

By Melanie Neilson

Pull up an archaic chair, overhear
Who first made the vinegar pie then was
Hungry bold with one eye on the sky.
Buttermilk day for blackberry night
Families, old marrieds, children, and friends
With time's pitter-patter in disguise.
Oh, the melodious group portraits vie
Others say did you hear or do tell
A ghost story or about the mountain
Observed traveling the Highlands of Scotland
Or how pie in the face vanquished the villain.
Nothing in dialogue with everything.
If we just had a vinegar pie, said the
Farmer, the lover, the baker, the poet
We would serve these beauteous battle pieces.
Tilly-hoo supper as birds begin to sing.

CLASSIC SOUTHERN PECAN PIE

MAKES ONE 9-INCH PIE;
SERVES 6 TO 8

From Cecile Richards

For the Crust

1½ cups (180 grams) all-purpose flour, plus more for dusting

3 tablespoons sugar

¼ teaspoon baking powder

¼ teaspoon fine salt

1 stick unsalted butter, cut into ½-inch pieces and chilled

1 large egg, lightly beaten

1 teaspoon pure vanilla extract

1 to 3 tablespoons ice water

For the Filling

4 large eggs

¾ cup sugar

½ teaspoon fine salt

1¼ cups dark corn syrup

1 tablespoon unsalted butter, melted

1½ teaspoons pure vanilla extract

1½ cups pecan pieces

Cecile Richards is a formidable progressive organizer, former president of Planned Parenthood, daughter of the iconic Texas governor Ann Richards, and a dynamic and inspiring leader. She is also the cofounder of Supermajority, a new home for women's activism: "One woman can be ignored, two can be dismissed, but together, we're a supermajority, and we're unstoppable."

Cecile is also an avid pie baker. This one is easy to put together, and sure to become part of your go-to repertoire.

Make the crust: In a food processor, pulse the flour, sugar, baking powder, and salt to combine. Add the butter and pulse until the flour looks powdery with pea-size bits of butter. Beat the egg and vanilla in a small bowl; add them to the flour mixture and pulse to combine. Drizzle in 2 tablespoons water and pulse until the dough just starts coming together but stop before it gathers into a ball. Grab a handful of the dough and press it together; if the dough is still very dry and crumbly, drizzle in 1 to 3 teaspoons of the remaining water. Wrap the dough in plastic or reusable wrap and refrigerate for at least 1 hour or up to 2 days.

On a lightly floured surface, roll the dough into a 13-inch round. Ease the dough into a 9-inch pie plate. Turn the edges of the dough over and under at the rim of the pie plate to make a double-thick edge. Crimp the edges as desired. Freeze until firm, about 15 minutes.

Position a rack in the lower third of the oven and preheat the oven to 350°F.

Make the filling: Whisk together the eggs, sugar, and salt, in a medium bowl. Add the corn syrup, melted butter, and vanilla and whisk until smooth and slightly frothy. Spread the pecans in an even layer over the bottom of the pie shell. Pour the filling over the nuts (they will rise to the top).

Bake the pie until the filling is firm and slightly puffed and the crust is golden brown, about 50 minutes. Let cool on a wire rack until set, about 30 minutes. Serve warm or at room temperature.

RICOTTA RICE PUDDING PIE

From Lisa Ludwinski

For the Crust

2½ cups (300 grams) all-purpose flour

1 teaspoon granulated sugar

1 teaspoon kosher salt

2 sticks unsalted butter,
cut into ½-inch cubes and chilled,
plus more for buttering

½ cup ice water, less 1 tablespoon

I tablespoon apple cider vinegar

For the Rice Pudding

¼ cup arborio rice

1 cup whole milk

⅓ cup heavy cream

4 teaspoons turbinado sugar
or light brown sugar

Pinch of kosher salt

½ teaspoon pure vanilla extract

1½ tablespoons unsalted butter,
cut into small pieces

The pies on display at Sister Pie, the beloved bakery in Detroit's West Village, look like the Thanksgiving dessert table you dream about all year. Sister Pie works to honor Michigan's seasonal food, as well as its community, employee empowerment, and community engagement. It's the kind of bakery that every town needs.

"My dad's side of the family is a 'sweets after every meal' kind of crew," owner Lisa says. "So his list of favorite desserts is long and varied. Growing up, our refrigerator was nearly always stocked with a pint container of Kozy Shack rice pudding. He'd scoop himself a little bowlful, sprinkled with a little cinnamon on top for punch. When it came time to turn that nostalgic and comforting treat into a pie, I also garnered inspiration from the traditional sweet rice pie made by Italian grandmothers for Easter celebrations. Fragrant with orange zest and rich with ricotta, this pie is light yet decadent and 100 percent Dad approved."

This all-butter crust, unlike some of the others you'll find in this chapter, is made by hand. The recipe makes enough for two piecrusts; freeze the other half. You'll be happy to find it in your freezer the next time you want to bake a pie. You'll also find that you have extra glaze; keep it in a jar in the refrigerator to use in cocktails and mocktails.

Make the crust: Combine the flour, sugar, and salt, in a large bowl. Place the butter in the bowl and coat all sides with flour. Using a pastry blender, begin to cut in the butter with one hand while turning the bowl with the other. It's important to not only aim to hit the same spot at the bottom of the bowl with each movement, but to actually slice through the butter every time. When the pastry blender clogs up, carefully clean out it out with your fingers (watch out, it bites!) and use your hands to toss the ingredients up a bit. Blend and turn until the largest pieces of butter resemble peas in size and shape.

continued

For the Ricotta Filling

4 large eggs, at room temperature

8 ounces ricotta cheese,
at room temperature

½ cup heavy cream,
at room temperature

¼ cup granulated sugar

1 teaspoon finely grated orange zest

1 teaspoon pure vanilla extract

⅛ teaspoon ground cinnamon

¼ teaspoon kosher salt

For the Citrus Glaze

¼ cup fresh lemon juice

¼ cup fresh orange juice

½ cup confectioners' sugar

Combine the water and vinegar; add to the flour mixture. Switch to a bench scraper and scrape as much of the mixture as you can from one side of the bowl to the other, until you can't see liquid anymore. Then, it's hand time: Using the tips of your fingers (and a whole lot of pressure), turn the dough over and press it back into itself a few times. With each effort, rotate the bowl and try to scoop up as much of the dough as possible, with the intention of quickly forming it into one cohesive mass. Remember to incorporate any dry, floury bits that have congregated at the bottom of the bowl. Once the dough is fully formed, it's time to stop!

Divide the dough in half, gently pat each portion into a disk, and wrap tightly in plastic or reusable wrap. Refrigerate for *at least* 2 hours, and ideally overnight. When you go to roll the crust, you want the disks to feel as hard and cold as the butter did when you removed it from the fridge to make the dough. (You will only need one disk, so freeze the other for up to 2 months.)

Liberally butter a 9-inch pie plate, leaving a 1-inch border unbuttered.

On a lightly floured work surface, roll the crust into a 12-inch round. Gently run your rolling pin over the entirety of the dough to make sure it's even. Place the dough in the prepared pie plate and then crimp the edges (see page 147 for more on crimping). Put the crust in the freezer for at least 15 minutes. (If you don't want to use it that day, allow the crust to fully freeze and then wrap it tightly in plastic or reusable wrap. It will keep for a couple of months in the freezer.)

When ready to bake the crust, set a rack in the lowest position in the oven and preheat the oven to 450°F.

Tear a piece of aluminum foil (a square slightly larger

continued

than the pie shell itself will work well) and gently fit it into the frozen crust. Fill the crust with dried beans (about 2 cups) and place on a baking sheet. Bake for 15 to 20 minutes, until the crimps of the crust are turning a deep golden brown. Remove the beans and foil and bake for 5 to 7 minutes more, until the bottom of the crust is set and very lightly browned. Transfer to a wire rack. Reduce the oven temperature to 325°F.

Meanwhile, make the rice pudding: In a small saucepan, combine the rice, milk, cream, turbinado sugar, and salt and bring to a boil over medium heat. Once it comes to a full boil—and be careful, this can happen within seconds—reduce the heat to low. Simmer, stirring occasionally with a spatula to prevent the bottom from scorching, until the rice is plump and tender, about 30 minutes. Remove from the heat, add the vanilla and butter, and stir until the butter has melted. Let cool completely; it will thicken up significantly as it cools.

Make the ricotta filling: In a large bowl, whisk together 3 of the eggs, the ricotta, cream, granulated sugar, orange zest, vanilla, cinnamon, and salt until very smooth. Fold in the cooled rice pudding with a rubber spatula until combined.

Assemble the pie: Put the piecrust on a baking sheet. Beat the remaining egg in a small bowl and brush the crimped edges of the crust with the egg. Pour the ricotta filling into the crust. Bake the pie until the edges of the filling are puffed and the center jiggles slightly when shaken, 50 to 60 minutes. It will continue to set as it cools. Set the pie on a wire rack and let cool completely, at least 2 hours.

Meanwhile, make the citrus glaze: In a small saucepan, combine the lemon juice, orange juice, and confectioners' sugar and bring the mixture to a rolling boil. Let cool.

Use a pastry brush to paint the cooled pie with some of the citrus glaze, then serve.

APPLE CHEDDAR SLAB PIE

From Katherine Alford

For the Cheddar Crust

3 cups (360 grams) all-purpose flour

1 tablespoon sugar

½ teaspoon fine salt

2 sticks unsalted butter,
cut into cubes and chilled

1 cup shredded sharp cheddar cheese
(about 3 ounces)

1 large egg, lightly beaten

¼ cup ice water

For the Filling

3 pounds mixed apples, such as
Cortland, Empire, Golden Delicious,
and McIntosh

Juice of 1 lemon

½ cup sugar

½ stick unsalted butter

1 tablespoon all-purpose flour

¼ teaspoon freshly ground nutmeg

1 large egg, lightly beaten

This pie works as a classic dessert, but it's just as welcome served alongside a juicy pork roast, or with wine and cheese. The best apple pies are made with a wide variety of apples, each adding their own special quality. For example, Golden Delicious hold firm during baking, Jonagolds and Granny Smiths bring tartness, and McIntoshes get saucy and mix and mingle to hold it all together. Check out local and heirloom varieties to make your own personalized combination. The cheese in this crust doesn't hit you over the head on the first bite but develops as you eat the pie. Choose an extra-sharp cheddar for a more upfront flavor.

Make the crust: In food processor, pulse the flour, sugar, and salt to combine. Add ½ stick of the butter; process until it disappears into the flour, about 30 seconds. Add the remaining 1½ sticks butter and the cheese and pulse until the mixture looks like cornmeal with bean-size bits of butter and cheese. Add the egg and pulse to combine. Drizzle the water over the flour mixture, then pulse until the dough just starts coming together but stop before it gathers into a ball. Turn the dough out onto a piece of plastic or reusable wrap and use it to press the dough together. Form the dough into a rectangle, wrap tightly, and refrigerate until firm, at least 1 hour or up to 2 days.

Meanwhile, make the filling: Peel, core, and slice the apples into ⅓- to ½-inch-thick pieces. Toss the slices in a large bowl with the lemon juice and sugar.

In a large skillet, melt the butter over medium heat. Add the apples and cook, covered, until softened and juicy, about 5 minutes. Uncover, stir once or twice, and cook until the apples are tender, about 10 minutes more. Scatter the flour and nutmeg over the apples and toss to combine; cook until the juices thicken, less than a minute. Let the apples cool completely.

Bring the dough to room temperature for 5 to 10 minutes, then divide it in half. On a lightly floured surface, roll one piece of dough into a 12-inch square. Transfer the dough to an 8- or 9-inch square pan and gently press it

continued

evenly over the bottom and into the corners of the pan, leaving the extra dough hanging over the edges. Brush with the beaten egg. Add the cooled apples, trim the edges of the dough, if needed, and fold about 1 inch of the dough over the apples. Refrigerate while you're rolling out the second piece of dough.

Roll the remaining piece of dough into a roughly 12-inch square, then trim it to a 10-inch square. Brush the part of the crust folded over the apple with more of the egg, then lay the dough on top of the apples and use a knife or small spatula to tuck the edges down between the bottom crust and the sides of the pan. If desired, use the excess dough to decorate the top of the pie. Freeze the pie for 15 minutes.

Position a rack in the bottom third of the oven and preheat the oven to 375°F. Put a baking sheet on the rack to preheat.

Place the pie on the preheated baking sheet and bake until the crust is golden brown, 45 to 50 minutes. Set the pie on a wire rack and let cool for 1 hour. Serve warm or a room temperature.

Despite It All,

By POLINA CHESNAKOVA

It was December 2016, temperatures were quickly dropping, and, as head baker at Greenwood Gourmet Grocery in Charlottesville, Virginia, I was tasked with making marshmallows for the shop's hot cocoa. Despite having never made them before, I knew exactly what I was aiming for: light and bouncy, heady with vanilla, a cloud of powdered sugar upon biting. My first trial, however, ended in disaster. Every surface was sticky with the meringue-like mixture, my arms were nicked with new burns, and the confections were setting out to be more tough and limp than soft and airy.

As I walked away in a huff, I felt a familiar vexing ember—the one that crept up when things weren't going my way in the kitchen. The only way to douse it was to throw more sugar at it until I nailed the recipe, and that small flame is what kept me from giving up. Little did I know the role that persistence would play in my life in the year to come.

The next morning, while driving to work (most likely thinking about those marshmallows), I lost control of my car on a gravelly, pothole-riddled road. I swerved up onto an embankment and into the air. At some point during one of the three flips, my left hand went through the window and was mangled and crushed beyond recognition. In the end, my surgeons were able to save it, but at the cost of two fingers and all hand function. It would be a long recovery, I was told, and the extent to which I'd regain use was uncertain. I didn't care, though. I was gifted a glimmer of hope.

That hope, however small, buoyed me through the numerous surgeries and around-the-clock pain during those first long winter months. I also grappled with a deep sadness that mostly expressed itself as rage. Not so much at what happened and the unfairness of it—I didn't let my mind go there—but that my ability to bake was stripped away from me.

I read cookbooks, scrolled through my social media feed, and watched *The Great British Bake Off*, and it left me wanting: for the feeling of cold butter giving under the pressure and heat of my fingers as I cut it into flour; the satisfaction of expertly tempering eggs and watching them thicken into a velvety smooth pastry cream on the stove; kneading dough into submission until my arms turned sore. I managed to pull off a few simple cakes with a stand mixer and nearby

Still a Baker

helpers, but it was a small reprieve—it didn't feel tactile and engaging enough. As long as my hand was clamped inside a giant splint or bandaged to the point that it looked like a large Q-tip, I was forced into a passive state that was at once exasperating and disheartening.

With the arrival of spring and summer, my bandages loosened, and at times, between surgeries, were shed completely. I rejoiced that I could *finally* get both my hands dirty and work out some of my anger. On one hand, every cake, cookie, and pie that I baked were indeed small victories, as well as my way of showing a big middle finger to the injustice of it all. *You can't stop me!* On the other hand, literally, I was missing fingers, and the ones that I still had were crooked and rigid from trauma and disuse.

Then one afternoon I felt brave enough to make a pie. I couldn't cut the butter quickly enough, so it kept getting too soft. I couldn't apply even pressure on the rolling pin, so the dough kept ripping and cracking. And without the pointer finger I usually used to make divots, my crimped edges looked like sloppy, half-hearted attempts. The pie eventually made it into the oven, but something about my rough assembly resulted in a third of the edge melting off halfway through baking. *This* from someone who once baked countless pies a day for a living. I sat on the kitchen floor and cried angry tears.

Looking back, I see that **rage baking saved me**. After the accident, it was my creative urge that drew me back to the kitchen, and it was rage that motivated me to return after, and despite, my failures. I believed that if I rolled out dough and separated eggs over and over, my left hand would eventually get the hang of it.

Physically and emotionally, baking did become easier over time. While my hand will never be 100 percent, thanks to countless surgeries and rehab sessions, it's pretty darn close. Those handicaps that once inspired despondent tears no longer exist in my eyes. But that vexing rage? Whether it's sputtering or roaring, it's always there, providing the push I need to keep going and fighting, even when I don't think I have it in me. I'm a baker—or, in other words, a perfectionist.

STRAWBERRY, MINT, AND LIME TART

From Katherine Alford

¾ cup sugar

¾ cup water

¼ cup lightly packed fresh mint leaves, torn, plus more sprigs for garnish

1 lime, zest removed in large strips using a wide vegetable peeler

Juice of 1 lime

1 sheet frozen puff pastry (about 7 ounces), preferably all-butter, thawed

All-purpose flour, for dusting

½ cup heavy cream

¼ cup plain whole-milk Greek yogurt or sour cream

2 cups strawberries, halved

What's in a name? A tart is really just a fancy pie. But call a woman a tart and it's an insult—floozy, loose, slut. A dictionary search of tart turns up "a woman who uses her sexuality too obviously." It's one of the many for-women-only labels. Bitch, witch, harpy, shrew, ballbuster—I've been called them all and own them with pride. This dessert is dedicated to women who are easy, sweet, loose, and tart. This tart is also "obviously" delicious—a lime cream spread on a pillow of buttery puff pastry with a cascade of juicy crimson berries. Any leftover mint syrup is great in iced tea or other drinks, or in your next berry tart.

Position a rack in the center of the oven and preheat the oven to 400°F. Line a baking sheet with parchment paper.

In a small saucepan, whisk together the sugar and water and bring to a boil over high heat. Reduce the heat to maintain a simmer and cook until syrupy, about 5 minutes. Off the heat add the mint and lime zest. Cool completely; add the lime juice. Strain into a liquid measuring cup.

Meanwhile, on a lightly floured work surface, roll the puff pastry into a 10 x 8-inch rectangle. Transfer it to the prepared baking sheet. With a pizza wheel or paring knife, score a rectangle in the pastry about ¾ inch from the edge on all sides— take care *not to cut all the way through*. Think of creating a picture frame. (Use a light touch; if you cut all the way, you won't get a beautiful rise.) Poke the middle of the pastry all over with a fork. Bake until golden brown, 25 to 30 minutes. Let cool for a few minutes. Take a small, sharp knife and gently recut the scored pastry. Cool completely. Lightly press down the center of the pastry to create a rimmed crust.

Whip the cream with an electric mixer on medium-high speed until it holds a slightly stiff peak. Add the yogurt and ¼ cup of the mint syrup. Beat again until the cream holds firm peaks. Refrigerate until ready to assemble the tart.

Spread the whipped cream evenly over the center of the crust. Toss the strawberries with 2 tablespoons of the syrup, then distribute them over the whipped cream. Tuck mint sprigs around the berries and serve immediately, or refrigerate for up to 2 hours before serving—any longer and the crust can get soggy, although it'll still be delicious.

SUMMER TOMATO PIE

From Katherine Alford

For the Crust

1½ cups (180 grams) all-purpose flour, plus more for dusting

1½ teaspoons minced fresh thyme (optional)

2 tablespoons sugar

½ teaspoon fine salt

1 stick unsalted butter, cut into small pieces and chilled

2 to 3 tablespoons ice water

1 tablespoon vodka (see Pie Tips, page 143)

Tomato pie is a Southern classic. Unlike quiche, which calls for a custard to hold the fillings, this pie relies on the very American mix of mayonnaise and cheese. I was suspicious at first, but then recalled all the delicious mayo-and-tomato sandwiches I ate as a kid. My version is sort of Tennessee meets Tuscany, with the addition of fennel and a mix of Italian cheeses. Although there are several steps involved in making this pie, if you prebake the crust, salt the tomatoes (essential to avoid a soggy pie), and caramelize the fennel and onion ahead, you can put the final pie together easily. Heads up: Your kitchen will smell like the best old-school pizzeria while this pie bakes.

Make the crust: In a food processor, pulse the flour, thyme (if using), sugar, and salt to combine. Add about one-quarter of the butter; process until it disappears into the flour, about 30 seconds. Add the remaining butter and pulse until the mixture looks like cornmeal with bean-size bits of butter. Combine 2 tablespoons of the water and the vodka and drizzle it over the flour mixture. Pulse until the dough just starts coming together but stop before it gathers into a ball. To see if the dough is moist enough, grab a handful of the dough and squeeze it; if it's still dry and crumbly, add 1 to 3 teaspoons of the remaining water. Turn the dough out onto a piece of plastic or reusable wrap and use it to form and press the dough together. Press the dough into a disk, wrap tightly, and refrigerate until firm, at least 1 hour or up to 2 days.

Meanwhile, make the filling: Line a baking sheet with paper towels and set a wire rack over the paper towels. Slice the tomatoes crosswise into ½-inch-thick pieces and lay them on the rack. Season both sides with salt. (This both seasons the tomatoes and concentrates their juices.) Let the tomatoes drain while you prepare the onions and fennel.

Heat 2 tablespoons of the oil in a medium skillet over

continued

For the Filling

1¾ pounds ripe heirloom tomatoes, mixed color and sizes

Kosher salt and freshly ground black pepper

3 tablespoons extra-virgin olive oil

2 medium onions, thinly sliced

1 medium fennel bulb, thinly sliced

1 garlic clove, minced

½ cup mayonnaise (olive oil–based ones are great for this)

⅓ cup shredded fresh mozzarella cheese (about 2 ounces)

⅓ cup shredded Parmigiano-Reggiano cheese (about 1 ounce)

⅓ cup shredded Pecorino Romano cheese (about 1 ounce)

¼ cup lightly packed basil leaves, minced, plus sprigs for garnish

medium-high heat. Add the onions and fennel and season with ½ teaspoon salt and some pepper. Cook, covered, stirring occasionally, until the vegetables wilt, about 15 minutes. Uncover, stir in the garlic, and cook, stirring occasionally to prevent scorching, until the vegetables have reduced in volume by more than half, about 20 minutes more. If the vegetables begin to stick to the pan, add a tablespoon or two of water. Let cool.

On a lightly floured surface, roll the dough into a 13-inch round. Place it in a 9-inch deep-dish pie plate; crimp the edges as desired (see page 147). Freeze until firm, about 15 minutes.

Position a rack in the center of the oven and preheat the oven to 400°F.

Line the crust with a piece of parchment paper or aluminum foil and fill with about 1½ cups dried beans, rice, or pie weights. Bake until the edges are just set and golden brown, about 15 minutes. Remove the parchment and weights and return the crust to the oven. Bake until the bottom of the crust sets and gets a little color, about 7 minutes more. Remove the crust and reduce the oven temperature to 375°F.

Whisk together the mayonnaise, cheeses, and basil, in a medium bowl, then evenly mix in the cooled onion-fennel mixture. Spread the mixture in the prepared pie shell. Layer the tomatoes on top, overlapping them as needed, drizzle with the remaining 1 tablespoon oil, and season with some pepper. Bake the pie until the tomatoes are slightly browned and the pie sets, about 45 minutes. Serve warm or at room temperature, garnished with basil sprigs.

MAIL-ORDER RAGE

Whenever possible, we like to buy locally at neighborhood shops. But when you need fresh fenugreek leaves or precut parchment paper or the perfect oven thermometer, you might not always find it close to home. Here are a few reliable mail-order companies we like to use for specialty ingredients and baking equipment.

ANSON MILLS
(ansonmills.com)
A leader in heritage freshly milled organic grains, offering everything from grits and cornmeal to a wide variety of flours like white bread flour, cake flour, rye flour, pastry flour, and more.

CAROLINA GROUND
(carolinaground.com)
Located in Asheville, North Carolina, Carolina Ground is devoted to growing Southern grains. They sell locally grown and ground bread flour, pastry flour, and rye flour. This is the rye flour that we used in Andrea Reusing's Rye Ginger Scones on page 46.

GRIST & TOLL
(www.gristandtoll.com)
This mill, co-owned by writer Marti Noxon (see page 15 for her interview), sells small-batch fresh-milled whole-grain flours. You can order from their collection, which includes hard white flour, Sonora flour, spelt, whole rye, cornmeal, and more.

KALUSTYAN'S
(kalustyans.com)
This New York specialty grocery is a great resource for specialty ingredients, flours, and chocolate. The spices and seasonings are particularly fresh, and you'll find everything you need for Indian-flavored baked goods and cooking. This is a good resource for dried fenugreek leaves (also called *methi*).

KING ARTHUR FLOUR
(kingarthurflour.com)
The go-to resource for all things baking: flour, equipment, baking classes, and tips. This is an employee-owned company of passionate bakers and one we are happy to support.

MICHAELS
(Michaels.com)
This huge chain store also offers online ordering and has reasonable prices on baking equipment and everything else a baker needs, from sprinkles, food coloring and gels, to gadgets.

NY CAKE
(nycake.com)
This is a great resource for everything you need for decorating, chocolates, flour, and equipment for enthusiastic home and professional bakers, as well as every color of sprinkles you can imagine.

PENZEYS SPICES
(penzeys.com)
Great resource for spices, spice blends, pure vanilla extract, vanilla bean paste, sea salts, and more.

WADE'S MILL
(wadesmill.com)
This is Virginia's oldest continuously operating commercial grist mill. They sell heirloom corn, wheat, buckwheat, and rye flours. They also offer the Bloody Butcher cornmeal we use on page 46.

ACKNOWLEDGMENTS

To all the women who contributed recipes, essays, poems, interviews, art work, we thank you. This is a collective in the truest sense of the word. When we wrote and told you about Rage Baking and asked you to be part of the project, you wrote back and said "Hell yes!" We are so deeply grateful.

To our agent, Stacey Glick, for shepherding this idea and getting it into just the right hands

To all the editors at Tiller Press. Our editor, Anja Schmidt, for your never-ending insight and support for this book, and all your great ideas and edits. To Theresa Dimasi for your enthusiasm for this project. To Patrick Sullivan, art director extraordinaire, for the thoughtful, brilliant design. To Ivy McFadden for the thorough copy editing. To W. Anne Jones for proofreading. Thanks to Jennifer Chung in the art department. Special thanks to Samantha Lubash and Matthew Michelman. To Marlena Brown, Erica Magrin, and Scottie Ellis for all help with publicity and marketing.

To Jerrelle Guy and her partner Eric Harrison for the gorgeous photography and understanding the recipes, stories, and vision of Rage Baking.

Kathy would like to thank John Rudolph for his never-ending support, love, and enormous appetite.

To Maya and Emma Rudolph for all the encouragement, edits, and love.

And to Katherine Alford, the best writing partner ever. Thank you for the friendship, the laughter, the dedication, the vision, the endless baking, and all those calories. You make life sweeter.

From Katherine: To Kathy Gunst whose passion for this project was an inspiration. I am forever grateful for your trust, insight, creative spirit, and the finest collaboration ever. I am blessed by the deliciousness of our friendship.

To Robert Johnson who makes life an adventure and who's steadfast encouragement is always touched with love, humor, and intelligence.

Thanks to:

Holley Atkinson

Chadwick Boyd

Stephanie Browner

Lyn and Harry Cason

Mary Cregan

Von Diaz

Anne Edelstein and Roy Moskowitz

EMILY's List, thanks to all the amazing women

Karen Frillmann

Aja Gair

Edy Getz

Dorie Greenspan

Paul Grimes

Fabia Hernandez

Asher and Robert Johnson

Elizabeth Kaplan

Lori Lordes

Tamar Martin

Ben Mims

Elisa Newman

Michael Portugal

Hali Ramdene

Julia Turshen

Joe Yonan

Keith Wasserman and Heide Feinstein

Aubin White

AUTHORS' NOTE

Molly O'Neill (1952–2019) was a special friend and mentor. She was a food writer, cookbook author, teacher, publisher, collaborator and inspiration to so many in the food and literary world. And, in many ways, she helped solidify the friendship between the two of us. Each September for several years, Molly hosted LongHouse, one of the most out-of-the-box food gatherings imaginable. Based on the nineteenth-century American Chautauqua movement, LongHouse was a weekend of eating, cooking, drinking, and finding new ways to talk about food and build community in a beautiful old red barn in a small town in upstate New York. We were both lucky enough to be part of the LongHouse events. The first year we attended, Molly arranged for us to stay in a guest house at the home of one of her local friends. We arrived late at night only to find that there were no sheets or towels. We snuck into the main house, which was dark and empty, snagged a few towels and sheets, and laughed like girls at sleep away camp. We were both recovering from cancer, another link in our friendship, and Molly somehow knew we were meant to be together. For that and so much more, we thank her.

Please follow us at ragebakers.com for news about signings and events. Follow us on Instagram @ragebakers and let us see your stories, your baking photos, and your rage.

CONTRIBUTORS

 **KATIE ANTHONY** has written about feminism and family for CNN, NBC News THINK, *BUST*, Scary Mommy, Upworthy, The Good Men Project, and others, but you can most often find her at her blog, *KatyKatiKate*. She lives outside Seattle with her husband and two sons.

 REEM ASSIL is the owner of Reem's California in Oakland, California, inspired by her passion for the flavors of Arab street-corner bakeries and vibrant communities surrounding them. Reem was a 2018 and 2019 James Beard Semifinalist for Best Chef: West, Star Chefs 2019 Rising Star Restaurateur, *San Francisco* magazine and Thrillest 2019 Chef of the Year, and *San Francisco Chronicle*'s 2017 Rising Star Chef.

 AMY BESA and her husband, chef Romy Dorotan, have been in the restaurant business in New York City for the past twenty-four years—first with Cendrillon, a Filipino Pan-Asian and now with Purple Yam in Brooklyn. Purple Yam Malate, in the Philippines, opened on July 4, 2014, in Amy's childhood home in Manila. Amy and Romy are coauthors of *Memories of Philippine Kitchens* (2006, Stewart, Tabori & Chang, NYC) that received the Jane Grigson Award for distinguished scholarship and writing by the International Association of Culinary Professionals in 2007.

 **BIANCA BORGES** has been cooking for a long time. Restaurant cook (1980s); pastry instructor at Peter Kump's New York Cooking School (1990s); food stylist for print and TV (among all the other stuff); culinary director of the *TODAY* show (2000s); TV cast and recipe development for Milk Street (now); myriad travel (always).

 JENNIFER FINNEY BOYLAN, the Anna Quindlen Writer-in-Residence at Barnard College of Columbia University, is the author of sixteen books, including *She's Not There* and *Good Boy.*

 **POLINA CHESNAKOVA** is a Seattle-based food writer, recipe developer, and cooking class instructor whose work has been featured in *Culture*, the *Washington Post*, *Saveur*, the Kitchn, and *Seattle Magazine*. Although she is no longer working in the kitchen professionally, she will always be a baker at heart.

 **VON DIAZ** is a writer and documentary film producer and the author of *Coconuts & Collards*. Born in Puerto Rico and raised in Atlanta, Georgia, she explores food, culture, and identity through memoir and multimedia.

 **ANI DIFRANCO** is a Grammy Award–winning songwriter, poet, rabble-rouser, and activist. She has produced more than twenty albums. She was born in Buffalo, New York, and lives in New Orleans. She is the author of the memoir, *No Walls and the Recurring Dream.*

CHARLOTTE DRUCKMAN is a journalist, food writer, and creator of Food52's Tournament of Cookbooks (aka The Piglet). She is the author of the books *Women on Food*, *Skirt Steak: Women Chefs on Standing the Heat and Staying in the Kitchen*, *Kitchen Remix*, and *Stir, Sizzle, Bake*, and the coauthor of Anita Lo's *Cooking Without Borders*.

KAREN DUFFY is a *New York Times* bestselling author and Pain Patient Advocate. Her love of baking was ignited when she plugged in her first Easy-Bake Oven. During her reign as the Coney Island Queen Mermaid, one of her duties was to jump out of a cake under the Coney Island Cyclone roller coaster.

NAOMI DUGUID is the author of *Taste of Persia* and *Burma* and the coauthor, with Jeffrey Alford, of six other books, including *Flatbreads and Flavors*, *Home Baking*, and *Hot Sour Salty Sweet*. She is currently working on cookbook tentatively titled *The Joy of Salt* for Artisan Books.

OSAYI ENDOLYN is a James Beard Award–winning writer who reflects on food, culture, and identity. Her work appears in *Time*, the *Washington Post*, the *Los Angeles Times*, Eater, and the *Oxford American*.

ELIZABETH FALKNER worked her way up in kitchens in San Francisco in the 1990s and owned and ran several restaurants through 2014. Today she does recipe development and consults for numerous products and brands and lives in Brooklyn, New York. She has appeared on more than forty cooking competitions on Food Network, Cooking Channel, Bravo, and NBC, appeared in many food magazines, and has received multiple awards, as well as a nomination for a James Beard Award (2005).

ANN FRIEDMAN is a journalist and host of the podcasts *Call Your Girlfriend* and *Going Through It*. You can find more of her pie charts at www.ann friedman.com.

MINDY FOX is a food writer, editor, cookbook author, and producer whose work has appeared in *Saveur*, *Food & Wine*, *InStyle*, *The Times* (London), Food52, Epicurious, and more. She lives in Portland, Maine.

BETTY FUSSELL, at ninety-two, is the author of thirteen books and winner of the 2018 James Beard Foundation Cookbook Hall of Fame award. She is best known for *The Story of Corn* and *My Kitchen Wars*. In 2017 she published her *Selected Essays: Eat, Live, Love, Die*, and is nearly finished with her second memoir, *How to Cook a Coyote*.

DARRA GOLDSTEIN is the founding editor of *Gastronomica: The Journal of Food and Culture*. Her new Russian cookbook, *Beyond the North Wind*, has just been published by Ten Speed Press.

DORIE GREENSPAN is the author of thirteen cookbooks, among them *Everyday Dorie*, *Dorie's Cookies*, and *Baking: From My Home to Yours*. She has won five James Beard Awards for her cookbooks and writing.

CARLA HALL is best known as a former cohost of ABC's Emmy Award–winning, popular lifestyle series *The Chew*. She currently appears on ABC's *Strahan and Sara*. She won over audiences when she competed on Bravo's *Top Chef* and *Top Chef: All Stars* and shared her philosophy to always cook with love. Carla believes food connects us all, and she strives to communicate this through her work, her cooking, and in her daily interactions with others.

JESSICA B. HARRIS is a culinary historian, cookbook author, lecturer, and consultant. Her work has been inducted into the James Beard Foundation Cookbook Hall of Fame.

PAM HOUSTON is the author of the memoir *Deep Creek: Finding Hope In the High Country*, as well as two novels, *Contents May Have Shifted* and *Sight Hound*; two collections of short stories, *Cowboys Are My Weakness* and *Waltzing the Cat*; and a collection of essays, *A Little More About Me*, all published by W. W. Norton. She teaches in the Low Rez MFA program at the Institute of American Indian Arts, is a professor of English at UC Davis, and is the cofounder and creative director of the literary nonprofit Writing By Writers. She lives at 9,000 feet above sea level near the headwaters of the Rio Grande.

PATI JINICH was born and raised in Mexico City. She is host of the two-time James Beard Award–winning PBS television series *Pati's Mexican Table*. Pati is also resident chef at the Mexican Cultural Institute in Washington, DC, and author of two cookbooks, *Pati's Mexican Table: The Secrets of Real Mexican Home Cooking* and *Mexican Today: New and Rediscovered Recipes for the Contemporary Kitchen*.

GENEVIEVE KO is the author of *Better Baking: Wholesome Ingredients, Delicious Desserts* and the cooking editor of the *Los Angeles Times*. She has written dozens of cookbooks with renowned chefs and created recipes for national media publications, such as the *New York Times* and *Better Homes & Gardens*.

VALLERY LOMAS is a lawyer turned baking blogger and food writer. She is best known for winning ABC's third season of *The Great American Baking Show* and has appeared on CNN, Fox, and the Hallmark Channel. She is currently working on her debut cookbook for Clarkson Potter.

LISA LUDWINSKI is the founder of Sister Pie in Detroit and the author of the cookbook *Sister Pie: The Recipes and Stories of a Big-Hearted Bakery in Detroit*. She lives a couple of blocks away from the bakery with her sweet pitbull, Ruby Thursday.

DOMENICA MARCHETTI is a cookbook author and food writer specializing in Italian home cooking. She writes for many publications such as the *Washington Post*, *Chicago Tribune*, *Cooking Light*, and others. She also runs workshops and tours of Italy.

KEIA MASTRIANNI is the baker behind Milk Glass Pie, a small-batch pie company based in Shelby, North Carolina. She bakes by the motto "Love is Pie."

ALICE MEDRICH is credited with popularizing chocolate truffles in the US in the 1970s. She has written ten cookbooks and won multiple James Beard Awards, and continues to influence and champion innovation and quality in the production of fine chocolate and confections in America. She is a regular columnist on Food52 and has a video class on Craftsy.com. Her most recent book, *Gluten-Free Flavor Flours*, explores the use of non-wheat whole-grain flours—with plenty of chocolate still involved!

PREETI MISTRY has been nominated twice by the James Beard Foundation as Best Chef of the West. She was the cofounder and executive chef of Navi Kitchen and Juhu Beach Club, as well as the coauthor (with Sarah Henry) of The *Juhu Beach Club Cookbook*. Born in London and raised in the United States, Preeti was a contestant on season six of *Top Chef*. Preeti and her restaurants have been featured in numerous publications, including *Food & Wine*, the *New York Times*, *Time*, *San Francisco Chronicle*, *Cherry Bombe*, *Wall Street Journal*, in addition to *Anthony Bourdain: Parts Unknown* on CNN. When

not running her restaurant, Preeti enjoys hiking, eating pizza, and growing veggies in her sunny Oakland backyard with her wife, Ann Nadeau.

MELANIE NEILSON is the author of four poetry collections. She cofounded and edited the radical small press writing journal *Big Allis* (1989–2000) in New York City with poet Jessica Grim. Born in Tennessee and raised in California, she lives in Queens, New York.

MARTI (MARTHA) NOXON is an Emmy-nominated writer and producer of the TV shows *Buffy the Vampire Slayer*, *Sharp Objects*, *Girlfriends' Guide to Divorce*, *Mad Men*, *UnReal*, and others. She is also a self-described "baking nerd" and co-owner of Grist & Toll, a grist mill in Pasadena, California, that specializes in locally grown wheat.

TESS RAFFERTY is a veteran television writer and the author of the memoir *Recipes for Disaster*, as well as the weekly cooking/political blog *Recipes for Resistance* (tessrafferty.substack.com). She is a regular contributor to *DAME Magazine* where she pens the She Is Running newsletter. Tess's video *Aftermath*, shot in the days following the 2016 election, has received more than 50 million hits on Occupy Democrats.

HALI BEY RAMDENE is a writer and editor interested in food, family, and well-being. She was formerly the food director at the KiTchn and a food editor at *Better Homes & Gardens*. She lives in Albany, New York.

RUTH REICHL was the last editor of *Gourmet* magazine. Her most recent book is *Save Me the Plums.*

ANDREA REUSING is the chef and owner of Lantern in Chapel Hill and the executive chef of the Durham Hotel in Durham, North Carolina. The recipient of the James Beard Award for Best Chef: Southeast in 2011, Reusing collaborates with small farms and producers across North Carolina and is an advocate for food policy change.

CECILE RICHARDS is a national leader for women's rights and social and economic justice, and a cofounder of Supermajority, a new organization fighting for gender equity. She is also the author of the *New York Times* bestseller *Make Trouble* and former president of Planned Parenthood Federation of America and Planned Parenthood Action Fund. In 2011 and 2012, she was named one of *Time* magazine's 100 Most Influential People in the World.

ELLE SIMONE SCOTT is the resident food stylist and appears on *America's Test Kitchen* on PBS and the first African American woman to do so. Elle has also been a stylist and culinary producer for Food Network, *Food Network Magazine*, Cooking Channel, CBS, ABC's *The Chew*, and Bravo. She is the founder and CEO of SheChef Inc., a professional networking organization for women chefs of color and allies. Elle shares her passion by mentoring, business development, and, most important, Food Social Justice.

MAXINE SIU was born and raised in San Francisco. She spent much of her life at her family's import/export business where she found her love of food. She and her husband and partner, Joel, are the couple behind the beloved San Francisco eatery Plow.

REBECCA TRAISTER is a feminist journalist and the author of *Good and Mad: The Revolutionary Power of Women's Anger.*

JULIA TURSHEN is the bestselling author of *Now & Again*, *Feed the Resistance*, and *Small Victories*. She is the founder of Equity at the Table (EATT), an inclusive digital directory of women/nonbinary individuals in food, and the host of *Keep Calm and Cook On*, a podcast.

VIRGINIA WILLIS is a James Beard Award–winning cookbook author, chef, and baker. She and her life partner, Lisa Ekus, are politically involved with organizations dedicated to resisting injustice, supporting civil rights, pro-LGBTQ+, environmental protection, alleviating hunger, reproductive rights, equal rights for women, and more.

GRACE YOUNG is known as the poet laureate of the wok, stir-fry guru, and wok therapist. When the news cycle gets too crazy, she relies on the basics—butter, eggs, sugar, chocolate—to bake something to soothe the soul and calm the spirit.

CREDITS

PHOTOGRAPHS

Katherine Alford by Robert Johnson; Kathy Gunst by John Hession; Alice Medrich by Deborah Jones; Amy Besa by Jar Concengco; Andrea Reusing by Lissa Gotwals; Ani DiFranco by GMDThree; Ann Friedman by Jorge Rivas; Betty Fussell by Amy Dickerson; Bianca Borges by Michael "Spyder" Clarke; Carla Hall by Melissa Hom; Cecile Richards courtesy of Cecile Richards; Charlotte Druckman by Melanie Dunea; Elizabeth Falkner by Cresta Kruger; Elle Simone Scott by *Boston Magazine*; Darra Goldstein by Stefan Wettainen; Dorie Greenspan by Ellen Silverman; Domenica Marchetti by Olga Berman; Genevieve Ko by Philip Friedman; Grace Young by Harrison Jeffs; Hali Bey Ramdene by Alicia Pender; Julia Turshan by Neal Santos; Jennifer Finney Boylan by Jim Bowdoin; Jessica B. Harris by Rog Walker of Paper Monday; Karen Duffy by Karim Chehimi; Katie Anthony by Mandee Rae; Keia Mastrianni by Rich Orris; Lisa Ludwinski by EE Berger; Marti Noxon by Patrick Harbron; Maxine Siu by SFGATE; Melanie Neilson by Dirk Rowntree; Mindy Fox by Christine Han; Naomi Duguid by Laura Berman; Osayi Endolyn by Lucy Schaeffer; Pam Houston by Mark Blakeman; Pati Jinich by Jennifer Chase; Polina Chesnakova by Kelsey Petrie; Preeti Mistry by Alanna Hale; Rebecca Traister by Victoria Stevens; Reem Assil by Jim Sullivan; Ruth Reichl by Michael Singer; Tess Rafferty by Justine Ungaro; Vallery Lomas by Neal Santos; Virginia Willis by Lisa Ekus; Von Diaz by Cybelle Codish

EXCERPTS AND OTHER MATERIAL

Page xii: US Supreme Court Building by Shutterstock.

Page 35: Women's March photo by Jim West / Alamy Stock Photo.

Page 52: *Good and Mad* by Rebecca Traister. © 2018 by Rebecca Traister. Reprinted by permission of Simon & Schuster, Inc.

Page 62: Challah recipe courtesy of Darra Goldstein.

Page 79: Adapted from *Baking from My Home to Yours*, published by Houghton Mifflin Harcourt.

Pages 136–137: Used by permission. Originally published in the *New York Times*.

Page 139: © 2019 by Ann Friedman.

Page 149: Flour photo by Shutterstock.

Kitchen utensils by Shutterstock.

INDEX

ABOUT THE AUTHORS

KATHY GUNST is a James Beard award–winning journalist and the author of fifteen cookbooks. Her most recent book is *Soup Swap*. She is the award-winning Resident Chef for NPR's *Here & Now*, heard on more than 550 public radio stations with more than 5 million listeners. She writes for many publications, including the *Washington Post*, *Eating Well*, *Wall Street Journal*, *Yankee Magazine*, the *New York Times*, *Food & Wine*, and others. Gunst teaches food journalism and cooking at schools and universities around the globe.

KATHERINE ALFORD ran the *New York Times*'s 4-star kitchen, the Quilted Giraffe, was a Greenmarket manager, as well as instructor and director of Peter Kump's New York Cooking School (now the Institute of Culinary Education). She spent the last twenty years at Food Network, ultimately as the Senior Vice President of culinary, where she led the culinary team for TV, digital, and print. She ran the test kitchen that created multiple cookbooks that were IACP award finalists, *Food & Wine*'s Best of the Best, and *New York Times* bestsellers. She oversaw recipe development and had a column in *Food Network Magazine*, the number one food magazine with a monthly reach of more than 1.3 million readers.